Churches That Heal

Churches That Heal

BECOMING
A CHURCH THAT
MENDS BROKEN HEARTS
AND
RESTORES SHATTERED LIVES

DOUG MURREN

Our purpose at Howard Publishing is to:

- *Increase faith* in the hearts of growing Christians
- *Inspire holiness* in the lives of believers
- *Instill hope* in the hearts of struggling people everywhere

Because He's coming again!

Published by Howard Publishing Co., Inc.,
3117 North 7th Street, West Monroe, Louisiana 71291-2227
99 00 01 02 03 04 05 06 07 08   10 9 8 7 6 5 4 3 2 1

Library of Congress Cataloging-in-Publication Data
Murren, Doug, 1951–
Churches that heal : becoming a church that mends broken hearts and restores shattered lives / Doug Murren
p. cm.
ISBN 1-58229-070-9
1. Church work. 2. Spiritual healing. I. Title.
BV4400.M85 1999
253—dc21   99-23968
CIP

Edited by Nancy Norris
Interior design by Stephanie Denney
Cover design by LinDee Loveland

Anecdotes in this volume are based on fact; however, in some instances details have been changed to protect identities.

Dedication

This book is dedicated to two very important people in my short little life.

First, to Vivian Brodine, my faithful assistant for sixteen years through thick and thin; I miss you. We fought some wars and saw a lot of healing.

Second, to my doctor, Dr. Ray Vath, who probably saved my life and taught me how to live again. He is a great healer.

CONTENTS

Foreword

BY GEORGE BARNA

How many people do you know who are hurting at a deep level? How many do you know who are struggling to understand the purpose of their lives or to achieve some degree of fulfillment in life by grasping its ultimate meaning? How many individuals can you identify who are struggling to overcome an addiction or to become integrated into the lives of other people? If you don't know anyone who fits these descriptions, you need to pay close attention to people's behavior and really listen their stories.

My research consistently shows that although America is currently enjoying a period of tremendous economic prosperity, unprecedented levels of interest in religion and spirituality, and a resurgence of interest in values and morality, tens of millions of people have been driven to such interest by the emotional, relational, and spiritual tragedies and emptiness they have experienced. For instance:

- More than seventy million adults are currently struggling to find meaning and purpose in life.

- More than twenty-five million people are profoundly lonely, and most of them are not elderly people living alone after the death of a spouse.
- More than fifty million citizens have endured the hardship of divorce, which exacts a toll on people's lives for years after the marriage is dissolved.
- More than twenty million adults have serious problems with gambling.
- An unknown number of adults and children suffer from physical abuse, typically at the hands of family members, and while estimates of such abusive behavior exist, they are almost certainly substantially lower than the reality.
- Substance abuse continues to plague the nation, with alcoholism on the rise and drug use stubbornly maintaining ground despite legislative and legal enforcement efforts to rid the land of illegal narcotics.
- The most frequent concern registered by teenagers and adolescents is that they do not receive unconditional love from their parents. This hardship afflicts an estimated two out of three kids between the ages of eight and eighteen in the U.S.

The examples could continue, but the point is unmistakable: A majority of Americans are seeking some form of healing in their lives, whether it be from physical addictions, unhealthy relationships, toxic spirituality, or other forms of hopelessness or unhealthiness.

But this raises the unavoidable question: Who will take the responsibility for reaching out to these people and trying to facilitate their healing process? We know it won't be the government. Businesses have tried to penetrate the market with a broad variety of approaches, products, and services; but many, if not most, of those have left people in even worse shape. The media are effective at reporting the disease but clueless regarding the solutions. Families are the ideal means through which such healing could be fostered, but few families are prepared to usher in healing solutions.

It appears that God's solution is, in fact, the best and most appropriate solution: The church must assume its role as the facilitator of such healing.

Consider our recent history in dealing with the many signs of need and unhealthiness. As a nation, we have tried a variety of solutions. We tried economic prosperity as the means to joy and fulfillment, but it left us emotionally and spiritually impoverished. We tried promiscuous sexuality, but it left us emotionally and spiritually drained. We tried to find meaning and purpose through career and achievement, but the result was an unsatisfying physical fatigue, family dissipation, relational emptiness, and spiritual hunger. We tried playing and partying in the hope that we could entertain ourselves into health and significance, but that also failed.

Ultimately, the only means to being a holistic, healthy individual is to be appropriately reunited with God. That means having an intense relationship with Jesus Christ and living life for the purposes of God. It means having a vibrant, growing connection with God's people through the instrument that he created to facilitate our joy, wisdom, and overall development. That instrument, of course, is the church.

But therein lies the rub. When you encounter friends who have deep emotional pain and need healing, to whom do you refer them?

Often, the church is not even on the list of possibilities that come to mind. When family members or neighbors confide in you about the suffering they are enduring and you realize that they are crying out for help, you may even love them so much that you go out of your way to protect them from churches. It is a sad commentary on the American church that we have become so acculturated that we have lost a tight, unyielding grip on the one imperative that must distinguish God's people from all other individuals, groups, and organizations: love. We preach the love game, of course, but we don't practice what we preach as often as we like to imagine.

Please do not make the grievous mistake, however, of believing that because we are not presently living up to our potential as agents of love, healing, and reconciliation that we cannot aspire to better things. That is where this book comes in. In a gentle, honest manner, Doug Murren reminds us of the unique calling of the church and gives us some guidelines on how to develop a church that can bring much-needed healing into the lives of the millions of people who desperately want a touch from God. God will deliver it through us if we are primed for the task.

I have had the privilege of knowing and ministering with Doug for more than a decade. I can assure you that few people have experienced such a roller-coaster ride with the church as Doug has. I've been there when he has been on top and when he has hit rock bottom. In some cases, the church demonstrated a tremendous healing touch that enabled him and the many who are affected by his ministry to be lovingly healed. In other cases, it has been the church itself, at its political and relational worst, that inflicted the wounds that would later require healing.

As I have studied churches and church leaders during the last twenty years, I have discovered that we can learn something from everyone. However, we can learn a lot more from those who have been through both the good times and the bad times, who have taken the time to assess their experiences, and who are willing to share their painfully gained wisdom with others. They have been trained by the toughest, most effective teacher available: experience. It's one thing to read about the ups and downs of life and to theorize about how you should cope with such challenges. It's another thing entirely to go through it all and to come out on the other end, bruised and battered but triumphant and ready to share the secrets of the journey with those who have ears to hear.

Doug has emerged from the trenches of ministry, bruised and battered but triumphant in Christ. He has led a church that has attracted and aided literally thousands of wounded people, bringing them to a better place through a spiritual journey that enabled the congregation to be the kind of healing salve that Christ intends us to become in this dangerous and wounded world. This book is Doug's way of sharing the key insights and lessons from his journey. I hope you have ears to hear. There is not much theory in this volume, and just as little overt theology. What Doug provides is a review of the hard-won lessons of life in light of God's mandate that his church be a place of safety for the scared, healing for the hurting, reshaping for the hurtful, and acceptance for the unloved.

This book addresses core issues related to the healing function of a church. There is a discussion about the importance of creating an environment in which healing can occur, the significance of personal responsibility in affecting others' lives, and the role of family in developing a church that does more than simply come together for an event every weekend. Doug's experience has helped him to emphasize the centrality of relationships in the healing process—just as the Christian faith is centered on an authentic, growing relationship with Jesus Christ. In chapter after chapter, you will read vignettes and nuggets of truth that will challenge some of your assumptions about ministry as well as spark new concepts of how to minister more effectively.

One of the most obvious and prolific themes of Jesus' ministry on earth was his healing of those who sought his help. His response to those in need of his touch is more than just good bedtime reading or an image-building library of stories. Jesus recognized that we have a substantial need to be healed—emotionally, physically, relationally, spiritually. His life was a model for us to emulate. The local church, as a group of Christ-lovers and Christ-imitators, must therefore demonstrate the healing touch too. Just as the evangelistic fields are ready for a major harvesting, so are the lives of Americans ready for a major healing touch by God, delivered through his people.

Do not turn your back on the need. And do not waste your time and energy seeking to reinvent the means by which churches can be agents of healing. Doug has done the homework for you. Read his words, analyze your ministry, pray for God's wisdom and blessing, and apply the insights necessary to convert your church into a haven of healing for the hundreds of people whose lives are influenced by those who call your church their spiritual base.

Acknowledgments

I want to acknowledge the great help that Michele Buckingham was in editing and redesigning many portions of *Churches That Heal.* Michele's wise input improved the book greatly. Her years as a senior editor for *Ministries Today* magazine have made her a pretty tough writing partner, but that's what makes for a good manuscript. I look forward to many more partnerships.

I also want to thank Marcus Maranto, who helped me get the initial presentation together. He, too, is very good at what he does.

My friend and advisor, Dr. Terry McQuirre, lent a lot of affirmation to the process and offered many careful insights that worked well here. Thanks for your confidence in my communication abilities.

INTRODUCTION

Restaking the Claim for Healing

Why should churches be places of healing? That's the question I got from several doctors when I mentioned the title of this book to them. We have modern medicine. We have great scientific understanding. We have new breakthroughs occurring nearly every day. Why in the world would churches want to get into the act?

In addition to conventional medicine, the New Age healing arts are deeply entrenched in my hometown of Seattle. Crystals, alternative therapies, mind/body science—with so many options available, who needs the church?

From all appearances, the church has been left out of the picture when it comes to healing today. The body of Christ has all but lost its claim to healing gifts that address the tangible needs of an ailing society.

I, for one, want to restake that claim.

One of my friends who is not a believer thought I was engaged in a very funny pursuit. "We all know why churches *should* heal," he said. "It's because people need healing! But can they do it? It seems to me that churches cause wars and make people ill by stifling creativity and fighting science. Maybe you should address those things, then come back and talk about healing."

While my friend's opinion of the church is somewhat jaded, he did hit on a key: *Churches should heal because people need healing!* That is the major reason any compassionate community of believers should want to create an environment where healing can take place.

And there's a higher reason: We want to heal because it glorifies God. Like worship, healing is a form of ministry to our heavenly Father, the Great Physician.

Healing can mean the mending of a body that is physically broken. It can mean the restoration of emotions that have been battered and bruised. But I have come to believe that the greatest healing next to salvation itself is the turning of a stony heart into a thankful heart. I want to turn your attention to a Scripture passage that we will refer to again and again. I call it "The Periscope of the One Healed Leper."

> Now on his way to Jerusalem, Jesus traveled along the border between Samaria and Galilee. As he was going into a village, ten men who had leprosy met him. They stood at a distance and called out in a loud voice, "Jesus, Master, have pity on us!"
>
> When he saw them, he said, "Go, show yourselves to the priests." And as they went, they were cleansed.
>
> One of them, when he saw he was healed, came back, praising God in a loud voice. He threw himself at Jesus' feet and thanked him—and he was a Samaritan.
>
> Jesus asked, "Were not all ten cleansed? Where are the other nine? Was no one found to return and give praise to God except this foreigner?" Then he said to him, "Rise and go; your faith has made you well." (Luke 17:11–19)

As I will explain later, I believe that thankfulness is the final act in a complete miracle of healing. So as you read on, read thankfully, and soak up anything that will help you make your own church a church that heals.

One Life Made Whole

I never had the opportunity to meet Corrine.

I did not know the pain she had suffered. Nor did I have any idea of the wonderful inner healing God had performed in her life through the services she attended at Eastside Church in greater Seattle, where I was pastor for sixteen years.

The first member of Corrine's family I met was her sister, Dorrine. I could see from photographs that she and Corrine were nearly identical twins, both blond and in their early thirties. My staff had filled me in on some of Corrine's story. But I wasn't prepared for what Dorrine told me, with tears in her eyes, the day she asked me to lead her sister's memorial service.

"Corrine thought so much of you," she said, gripping my arm. "She said she would never have gotten sober if she hadn't found this church, if you weren't her pastor." She explained that through one of the twelve-step programs at our church designed to help hurting people grow spiritually, our leaders had shown Corrine true, unconditional love.

Dorrine began to cry. "She knew she was going to die, you know," she said.

Puzzled, I asked, "What do you mean?"

"Last Monday, we attended the outreach meeting where you taught on life after death and Ricky Skaggs sang," she said. "Corrine was so happy. She'd only known the Lord for six months. Those were the richest six months we ever had together as a family."

"That sounds like a wonderful gift," I responded.

"When she came home that night after the event, she said she knew for certain now that there was life after death and that she was going to heaven to serve Christ. Then she turned to me and said, 'Make sure that Pastor Doug does my funeral.'" Dorrine paused and gently wiped her eyes before continuing. "She said, 'I want to be remembered in that church, because I've sensed God there so many times.'

"You know, Pastor, I told her to stop talking like that. She was young—only thirty-one years old! But she insisted. In fact, she made the whole family promise her that if she died, we would attend Eastside in memory of her and would receive the Lord. Pastor, she could be feisty, and we all agreed we would."

Then Dorrine, finally overcome with grief, couldn't speak anymore. I was glad to have heard more about her sister. I assured her that I would consider it a great honor to lead Corrine's memorial service.

Later that day, I heard the rest of the story from Corrine's mother. For nine years Corrine had been a drug addict, totally lost to her family. Then she'd gotten sober, found Christ, and was wonderfully healed. Corrine's family had never seen her as happy as she was in those last months, when she was a part of our church family. In fact, her mother said to me, "She was really being healed from the inside out."

As it happened, Corrine and Dorrine had attended one of our church's quarterly Monday night outreach meetings. At these events, the regular attendees in our congregation invited skeptics and cynics to come and have fun while hearing a presentation of the gospel suited perfectly to them.

The next night, Corrine went to the Alcoholics Anonymous meeting at the church. Her ride home was late, so she set out on foot. As she walked beside the road about half a mile from our building, she was struck by a driver who didn't see her. Corrine was killed instantly.

If Corrine's death seems tragic, the story of God's redeeming and healing work in her life through the people at Eastside Church is truly inspiring. I have made it my personal quest to discover the conditions under which people like Corrine can experience God's wonderful acts of healing in their lives.

A Healing Environment

I have become convinced that God uses the church's environment, as much as our prayers, to bring healing. Not all churches have an environment that is conducive to healing. There are many "toxic" churches today—communities where guilt, manipulation, fear, and shame reign, poisoning the spiritual atmosphere and making healing all but impossible.

What traits can churches aspire to that will allow them to avoid these toxins? How can we build churches that heal?

Through extensive study, prayer, and practice, I've identified what I believe are the main characteristics of healing churches. I share these characteristics with you as a fellow journeyer in the Spirit who longs to see more true healing taking place in the church today.

I am a pastor, an evangelist, and a leader. But I'm not a theologian. Thus, in this book, I will not give you a theological treatise. Instead, in the process of looking at biblical texts and sharing true stories, I hope to give you practical knowledge and skills that will help you create a church that can actively bring healing to your community.

I encourage you to read this book with an attitude of openness, appreciating whatever benefit it offers you while having patience with any shortcomings you may detect. If you have this attitude, you may find that you are being healed as you read.

And that's important—because in order to develop a healing church, we, as "wounded healers," must be willing to acknowledge the toxins in our own lives that could affect the healing environment we seek to create.

Ultimately, the best healers are the ones who've experienced their own pain. It's like having a doctor who has the same disease you do; you realize he probably knows more than just what the books have to say, and that makes you more open to his diagnosis and treatment.

So, from one wounded healer to another, let's discover how we can begin to develop churches that heal.

You don't build a wall a mile at a time. You build it a brick at a time.

———— ■ ————

Fern Murren (my granddad)

1

Why Churches Don't Heal

Several years ago, I performed my last baptismal service—not because I don't love sharing such a joyful time with new believers, but because our church leadership decided that laypeople would begin officiating at baptisms. Pastors don't have to do everything!

I vividly remember that particular morning. The last person to be baptized was an attractive twenty-three-year-old named Cathy.

"How long have you been attending Eastside Church?" I asked her as we stood before the congregation.

She smiled and leaned into the microphone. "Two years," she said.

"And when did you receive Christ?"

She let out a high-pitched laugh and responded, "Just last week!"

As I baptized her, I couldn't help but wonder to myself, *Why did it take two years?* Afterward, I hurried back to catch her as she emerged from the changing room in dry clothes, a towel draped around her head. Cathy was typical of the kind of people our church was trying to reach. I knew there were things I could learn from the experience of this joyful new believer.

"Cathy, can I speak with you for a moment?" I asked.

"Sure, Pastor." She politely sat down.

"You said you have attended Eastside for two years. I am interested in finding out: Have you been coming just once in a while, or have you been here every week?"

"Oh, Pastor, I have attended almost every week. I love the music, and your messages always help me get closer to God. Why do you ask?" She looked at me with brown, doe eyes.

"Well, Cathy, why did you wait two years to receive Christ? I want to learn from your experience."

Cathy hesitated for a moment as she collected her thoughts. "Pastor Doug," she began, "I was really hurting when I came to Eastside. I had had three abortions by the time I was twenty-one. I knew that was wrong. And I had also just quit drinking. I realized I needed God; I just didn't know how to find him.

"My parents were Christians—that is, until I was in seventh grade," she continued. "Then they lost their faith and got a divorce. So when I realized I had to make a big change in my life, I went to live with my grandparents, who were Christians. They really helped me. They even told me not to come to their church, which they had attended for years, because they were sure I would feel even worse there!

"They told me to come to Eastside Church, because they knew I would be loved here. Pastor, it took two years for me to truly see that you were for real. Now I know even more than that: I know that Jesus is real in my life." As she finished, a big, beautiful smile came over her face, revealing the deep joy and healing she had found.

And I couldn't help but smile too. With the guidance of her grandparents, Cathy had found a church environment that had not only given her an awareness of God's love, it had ministered the personal healing she so desperately needed.

Trying Too Hard

I think Americans still secretly hope that the church is all she says she is. When a crisis hits, many people still think first of going to a pastor to receive consolation and help. In more than two decades of pastoring, I have often received phone calls from people who have never been to church yet want me to pray for them for healing or strength in a severe life challenge. I'm convinced that despite a documented slide in the popularity of true, biblical Christianity in America, your neighbors and mine are secretly hoping that we still believe Christ's grace is sufficient to heal them.

But what happens when people in need of healing arrive at church? Do they find an environment that demonstrates God's unconditional love and promotes personal healing? Too often, they do not.

Why not? Why is the formerly suicidal new believer simply dumped into a position of service rather than placed under the care of a wise leader who can help him rebuild his broken life? Why is the unique, creative individual treated like a misfit rather than helped to find out where she fits best in the body of Christ? Why is the confused teenager, pregnant with her father's child, shamed in front of the youth group so that she becomes bitter and resolves to never again attend church?

Sometimes our churches don't heal because we simply try too hard. This may seem like a surprising statement since we know that many churches make no effort and place no priority on personal healing. But often, in churches that want to heal, we try too hard; we take our church roles too seriously.

I am convinced that Jesus' inclination to attend parties shows us what church should be: a joyful group of people partying with the most unsuspecting types.

Jesus would probably have declined an invitation to your home or mine in order to keep a social engagement with Jack Kevorkian or John Gotti and his friends. He would have visited with O. J. Simpson or spent the weekend matching wits with students at a notorious fraternity.

Jesus still likes a good party! But too often we in his church get so overly serious about ourselves and so zealous about our mission that we end up crushing those we are trying to help. We drown them with wordiness; we prescribe too many prohibitions that benefit no one.

The Holy Spirit can turn joy and fun into holiness much more readily and quickly than he can transform living by rules. Take Zacchaeus's moral and ethical healing in Luke 19:1–10, for example. Jesus could have lectured Zacchaeus in the street about his crooked business practices. Instead, the Lord risked his own reputation by going to the tax collector's home for a party.

No doubt Jesus had a good time in Zacchaeus's house. And by the end of the festivities, Zacchaeus announced that he was going to follow Jesus, give half of his possessions to the poor, and pay back four times anything he had stolen from anyone!

With this in mind, I think every church should place the following words at the top of its weekly bulletin: Lighten up in Jesus' name! As surprising as it may sound, fun—that is, carefree enjoyment or playfulness—is a necessary characteristic of the Holy Spirit's healing presence. Yet most of us take the opposite track. We try hard to be "righteous" enough to bring healing to people, but that very effort works strongly to prevent the healing we strive so hard to promote.

Broken people see through these labored exertions. They know that being good isn't enough to bring healing. They've already tried it.

We also tend to talk too much. We can't heal others if we don't listen to God first! Even Jesus said he could only do what he saw the Father doing (see John 5:19). Nor can we make others feel loved unless we listen to them. St. Francis of Assisi was at the peak of his genius when he personalized the Great Commission for us, saying, "Go into all the world and preach the gospel. And use words if you have to."

Watching Seeds Grow

Let me tell you a modernized version of a Native American tale set in the woods of the American Northwest.

A raccoon and a possum met and soon became good friends. One day the raccoon invited the possum to his home near the river. When the possum saw a beautiful garden outside the raccoon's home, he was envious. "Could I have a garden like this?" he asked.

"Why, of course, anyone can," the raccoon answered. "It's hard work though."

"I will work hard! Give me some seeds," the possum said.

"Okay, here is a bag of seeds. Just throw them on the ground and bury them, and they will grow into a beautiful garden like mine," the raccoon instructed.

So the possum ran home as fast as he could with the bag of seeds in his hand. When he arrived he took a spoon and dug out the seeds. He threw them all around, laughing and dancing. Then he covered them with dirt.

Afterward, the possum went into his house, ate a cheese sandwich, and fell asleep. When morning came, he jumped out of bed and ran outside. But to his amazement, there was no garden! Anger welled up within him. He began pounding the ground and screaming, "Grow, seeds, grow!"

Animals and birds from throughout the forest gathered to see the possum rage. The possum's raccoon friend was among the spectators.

The raccoon spoke up. "What are you doing, Possum? Your racket has awakened the whole forest," he scolded.

"I have no garden. I tell the seeds to grow, but they do not grow," the possum answered, and he demonstrated by stepping from seed to seed and thundering, "I command you to grow!"

All the animals began making fun of the possum for thinking he could make seeds grow by yelling at them. But the possum only yelled louder.

Finally, the raccoon could stand it no longer. "Hold on now, Possum," he said. "You can't make the seeds grow. You can only make sure they get sun and water, then watch them do their work. The life is in the seed, not in you."

The crowd dispersed, and from that point on the possum began watering the seeds regularly. Sometimes, though, when the other animals weren't around, he still did a little shouting.

Finally one morning the possum awoke to see that his garden was full of beautiful green sprouts. Just a few days later, flowers began to bloom.

He ran and asked the raccoon to come and enjoy his garden with him.

The raccoon was pleased. "You see, Possum, all you had to do was let the seeds do their work while you watched."

"Yes," smiled the possum knowingly. "But it is a hard job watching a seed work."

There's a lesson there for all of us. Sometimes, as Christians and church leaders, we work too hard and take ourselves too seriously instead of simply planting people in the proper environment and letting them grow.

I remember a couple whose son was diagnosed with severe asthma. Desperate for help, they attended a "healing conference" where they were taught a seven-step process for receiving healing. As they described it to me, I couldn't help but think that the process resembled New Age chanting more than anything remotely biblical.

The family tried hard to use this process. It seemed to them a great failure and a lack of faith on their part when they finally had to give in and put their son on the medication prescribed for his condition.

"Would you pray that our faith would increase?" they asked me.

"No," I said, to their surprise. "Instead, I prescribe a celebration. Thank God for the medical discoveries that have provided effective medication to help your son. Your faith will grow as you become thankful to God. Don't try to make a miracle or healing happen—just enjoy God and celebrate that he cares."

They promised to do just that, and we prayed accordingly. No immediate miracle took place, but their journey to healing became filled with joy, and the illness was eventually checked.

Both the Bible and medical science agree: Joy is good medicine! I'm convinced healing can only be realized as we approach God with joyful hearts and release our problems to the One who cares so deeply about us.

A Place of Acceptance

Even if churches don't try too hard, they still may not bring healing. Often the church is just not a safe place for us to let down our guard and be real. Imagine needing urgent medical care and going to a hospital where you dare not admit that you have been injured! Similarly, it often seems that the last place we can admit to a personal struggle is in the church. And so we are not healed, and we do not heal others.

One Saturday afternoon, as I walked the halls of our church praying for the celebration service that would be held there that evening, the phone began to ring at the reception desk. A volunteer's voice rang out from the other end of the hall, "Pastor Doug, could you answer that for me? I'll be there in a minute." I was glad to do it.

"Hello, Eastside Church. Can I help you?"

"Yes, who am I speaking to?" a quiet voice asked on the other end.

"This is Pastor Doug Murren. Can I help you?" I repeated.

The man on the other end paused, then began to cry. "Can I come to church if I have been divorced? I have to find God."

"You're welcome here, no matter what!" I assured him.

Unchurched people today often feel that we don't like them—that we don't want them around. Yet they hope we will. They want to be healed!

Of course, no church is ever a perfectly healing church. All churches are a mixture of healing and toxicity—hopefully, more healing than toxic. Even churches that heal don't get it right every time. A vision to heal is like the buoys that mark the channel to a port.

You know the way to go, and when you fail, you know how to return and get back on course. If there is no thought given or plan implemented to promote healing, churches can get off track and drift off into toxic waters. But we know where to return when we find ourselves failing: to the incarnate, forgiving, divine healer, Jesus Christ.

This is a great comfort to me because I have so often failed at what I preach that sometimes I have just wanted to give up.

In the seventies, I worked twice a month with the chaplain of Washington State Penitentiary. Through an unexpected turn of events, I was offered the opportunity to meet regularly with the death-row inmates.

I got to know three of the inmates quite well. One was an eighteen-year-old biker who had taken the life of a teenager whose leather coat he wanted. Another had murdered his wife and her lover. The man I came to know most closely was named Tom; he had robbed and killed two elderly women to get money for heroin.

Of the three, all but the biker became Christians. Eventually the death penalty was dropped in Washington State, and these inmates were released into the general population.

I had neither seen nor thought of these men for twenty years. Then one Sunday morning, as I was praying with people and giving counsel in the front of our church auditorium, I saw Tom with his new wife. I am sure my face drained of color. I felt nothing but fright at seeing this man—he was a murderer, after all!

Tom and I chatted briefly and cordially. He asked me to go to lunch with them, but I politely turned down the offer. I knew the only reason I refused was that I didn't want Tom to feel connected to me. I was sure it would be a big job to have him around, and I was so overloaded already—at least, that's how I justified my behavior to myself. I am still ashamed as I think about it today! Clearly, my tone and body language communicated, "I don't accept you. I can't get beyond your past."

I wasn't a healer that day. I looked for Tom and his wife in the congregation for weeks afterward, but they never returned. This man had taken the risk of reaching out in my direction, and I had let him down. Oh, Jesus, forgive us our failures! That one failing drove me to my knees and back to the most basic foundation of Christian ministry: love, acceptance, and forgiveness in Christ.

Churches that don't heal, frankly, sometimes don't want to deal with the mess of broken lives seeking help. What are we afraid of? We need to ask God to heal us of our fears!

MAJORING ON NEGATIVE EXPERIENCES

I have not always found church to be a friendly environment—neither as a young layperson nor as a pastor for nearly thirty years. As one friend of mine says, "Doug, there's a lot in the church that isn't in the Bible, and there's a lot in the Bible that isn't in the church."

I have experienced betrayal; I have been misunderstood; I've been robbed; I have been libeled deliberately; I have felt so very alone in the midst of the fight—even as I was giving my all to the church. I have been bitter many times, convinced the church no longer had much to offer me. In that, I've not been alone. I'm aware of many, many pastors and leaders who are cynical about the church.

At the same time, I've had to admit that my pain has never matched what Christ has suffered at my hand in betrayal, denial, and disobedience. And I've recognized that if I stack up all my negative church experiences against all the wonderful experiences and kind treatment I have known in the body of Christ, the good outweighs the bad five hundred to one.

Some of the greatest betrayers I know are church members. But despite their presence, the church continues to produce a myriad of the kindest and most generous people on the planet.

My wife says I am kind of eccentric. I am not a good executive-type pastor. My personality type, the way my brain works, and the fact that I have conquered bipolar disease have caused my perspective to be quite different than others'. I have been hurt by people who have been quick to label me as a "this" or a "that." As far as I know, all I have ever been is Doug.

At times I've struggled to come to grips with the imperfect church Jesus has created. My doctor, a great friend and Christian, gave me this advice: "Stop whining! You can't control what happens to you most of the time. But you can always choose your response." Our response is what determines whether we will become bitter leaders or healing leaders.

The Bible portrays the greatest leader of all time in numerous bitter states. King David was often depressed, agitated, and incensed by the mistreatment he endured. But every time David went into a diatribe about his poor treatment at the hands of others, God would answer, in effect, "David, hush. Those guys may be jerks, but you can be a jerk sometimes too! I'll deal with the right guys at the right time. You just praise me and work on your own heart."

I choose not to rehearse some of the pain I have been through—mainly because I don't understand the complex issues well enough to pop off about anyone else. Trust me: I have been hurt deeper than deep by Christian leaders and followers in several church organizations. But I've always found that a healthy perspective is recoverable—often after a long period of contemplation and prayer and, quite frankly, sometimes after months of bitterness and even anger at God. Today I can thank God for every organization I belong to or have ever belonged to. Really.

It is never right to keep quiet about grievances in the face of real abuse. Growth, for everyone involved, only occurs when we face tough issues. After months of misunderstanding and agony, one organization that had hurt me turned around and treated me with such kindness that I felt like I saw more of God in one afternoon than I might have in years. I saw that organization struggling to be what it was really supposed to be, and it succeeded! In the process, I was healed.

My doctor friend knows what he's talking about: Our responses to painful circumstances help determine our lives. Looking back, I can see clearly that God has used my negative experiences to direct me. And I can also see that any loss I have experienced in God's work over the last twenty-five years has always been returned to me double. By grace, I have moved from bitterness to acceptance to openness to effectiveness.

If you are a leader, you have almost certainly had to undergo some of what I have undergone in the process of leading. I sense such pain in many of the places I go. But pain produces patience and grace. Until you have hurt, you will not be able to help those who do.

At a recent conference, I was approached by a man who mentioned that he had heard me speak a number of years earlier—long before I had been slapped around a bit. "Doug, you were very good at communicating back then," he said, "but you had an edge—as if you thought you had the world by the tail. But when I heard you today, I sensed you were not just a communicator anymore. I sensed you had gone through something in the last four years that has produced a certain tenderness. When you spoke this time, I felt you understood our challenges and really cared for us as leaders and people."

His wife added, "Your eyes even look different now—kind of happy-sad."

They were nice people, and they had hit upon something true. I had been softened greatly by the difficult experiences of the preceding years. Pain leads you to see what is really important in a way success never can.

Following is a checklist I now go through to make sure I'm responding well whenever I'm faced with painful circumstances. To be honest, sometimes I don't remember to pull it out until I've gone through a few days of "mad"—but late is better than never.

- Be honest about abusive treatment. Meet the person face to face who has harmed you and tell the truth. His response is up to him.
- Be responsible with your assignments. Twice I have stayed on six months after resigning to make certain that I, at least, had made credible efforts to improve a negative environment.
- Don't give in to fear. Be led by God's promises, not your fear of what may happen.
- Do not retaliate, and remember that God may not either.
- Take note of the number of times you have been just as bad as the people who hurt you.
- Forgive. Let people become more than what they do wrong.
- Look to the future; don't rehash the past.
- Thank God for the good experiences you have had.
- Don't bad-mouth the ones who've hurt you.
- Find your new direction. Remember, God uses negative experiences as a guide.

I've found that churches led by boards, congregations, or ministers who've taken on a cynical and accusatory attitude toward church experience never heal others. Healing churches are those who have processed the mistreatment.

The Danger of Folk Theology

Christians often rally to what I call "folk theology"—beliefs that sound spiritual but are actually based on overly simplistic explanations and solutions for life's problems. This kind of theology works dramatically against the healing process.

Here's a common statement from folk theology: "If you have emotional issues in your life, the problem is really spiritual." Why is this so dangerous? Because we know that many emotional disorders stem from brain injuries and chemical malfunctions in the brain. It is more likely in many cases that brain malfunctions are causing spiritual problems, rather than the other way around. Telling someone their problem is spiritual when it's not can send them on a wild goose chase and keep them from pursuing the kind of help they really need.

Here's another one: "If you have problems in your marriage, it's because Satan is attacking your home." I think at times this can be true. But most couples I know need a good course on communication more than a good fight with the devil.

There is a simple way to live. But there are no simple answers. When it comes to healing, overly simplistic ideas from faulty folk theologies can do more harm than good.

Leaders can be particularly damaged. In churches that rely on folk theology, pastors or board members who admit to emotional, marital, or family problems are often quickly shown the door. It shouldn't be that way. Leaders who are allowed to have problems, who are encouraged to work through reasonable issues with the support of the church, can become models of how God works on our behalf.

Of course, leaders don't have to have problems to be effective. But struggles with health, family, and church issues can be used by God to develop sensitivity and increase leadership skills.

Wisdom is necessary here. While it is faulty to deny problems, I made the mistake a couple of times of making my issues too much a focus for the church. Sometimes the challenges we are going through are best shared when they are over.

I struggled for five years to decide whether to tell my congregation that I was bipolar. Through the help of a great Christian doctor, the blip in my brain chemistry was being treated and my manic-depression was well under control. But I finally had to address the church because rumors had begun to circulate that exaggerated the real nature of my challenge.

Speaking up was the right thing to do, but my announcement was poorly timed, and I tried to be flippant. Hundreds of people were helped by my openness, but hundreds were also frightened. It was a tough situation. I think that if I had had the right kind of support, the whole thing could have been handled better than it was, and we could have moved on more quickly. That's why I feel strongly today that leaders must have networks of peers who will walk with them through the unavoidable challenges of life and ministry.

Churches that heal must accept and deal with humanity's challenges. They must approach the difficulties of life with an attitude of love. Our fears are the great enemies to our healing gifts. I feared the man who was a murderer, and I failed to heal. My bipolar disorder seemed frightening to others, and so I was misunderstood. In these examples, fear brought failure to heal even in the lives of people who were fully devoted to being healers.

Every decision we make as Christians is driven by one of two motivations: fear or the power of God's love in us. Fear was the reason for the first sin. Adam and Eve feared God was withholding something important from them, and so they ate the forbidden fruit. When churches live in fear, they destroy leaders, and they send away broken people.

The apostle John wrote, "There is no fear in love. But perfect love drives out fear" (1 John 4:18). As we move through life and its many problems drawing upon God's perfect love, that love will drive out all fear, and we will heal.

HEALING TAKES RISKS

The women in the Murren household have forced me to sit through several viewings of the movie *Thelma and Louise*. This film is the fictional story of a woman who is nearly raped during a secret night out on the town; the attacker is shot point-blank by the woman's girlfriend, who comes upon them in the parking lot.

From that violent incident, the two women, filled with terror and anger, set out on a multistate crime spree. Everywhere they go, men are made to suffer horribly.

In the movie's final scene—the most powerful I have seen in the last decade—scores of police cars converge on the area where Louise's car is parked, near the edge of the Grand Canyon. Sirens blare. Rifles are drawn. Machine guns are poised and ready. Helicopters with sharpshooters dangling from the open side prepare to forcibly end the vengeful women's violent spree.

The women weigh their plight carefully. Their car has been a symbol of escape and safety to them. Now it is all they have left. Without a word they join hands, back the car up as far as they can, stop, then quickly accelerate toward the edge of the gorge. They reach the precipice, then dramatically plunge toward the bottom. They are free!

Today, people like Thelma and Louise are running scared, and they face an unspannable chasm. In our society, an existential leap into oblivion is often seen as the only path to freedom from the pain of failed lives.

Some, however, drive to the edge of the gorge, then lunge back toward the church for freedom and healing. That is what I did. But too often, when they make that lunge, the church fails to reach out and hold them long enough to heal.

So they remain on the verge. Prisons grow more crowded. Drug use increases. Violence and racism continue to embitter many. Revival wanes. And the world becomes a worse place to live.

Heal us, Lord, and we shall be healed;
save us and we will be saved;
for it is you we praise.
Send relief and healing
for all our diseases,
our sufferings and our wounds;
for you are a merciful
and faithful healer.
Blessed are you, Lord,
who heals the sick.

———— ■ ————

Traditional Jewish Prayer

2

What Happens When Churches Don't Heal

It is easy for most of us in church leadership to assume that our church is healing people. In fact, every church does have a measure of healing taking place all the time. After all, wherever Jesus is worshiped and his presence is celebrated, healing is likely to occur.

But what if, more often than not, the church we lead *doesn't* heal? We must be willing to take a hard look and ask: Are there traits within our church that violate the basic principles for healing others? Have we set boundaries limiting the kinds of healing Christ will do?

The first step to becoming a church that heals is to pause and seek answers to these and similar questions. We must discover and address every attitude and practice that blocks healing. Let me introduce you to a few victims of churches that failed to take this critical step.

A Pastor Thrown Off Course

I'd never met Fred before, though I probably had crossed paths with him a time or two at some pastoral functions in our community. He and his wife and two children found their way to the front of the sanctuary after one of our services. His eyes had dark blue rings under them, betraying a wounded spirit. His wife appeared to be in better condition—but not by much. The kids were happy-go-lucky, as kids will be. I learned that a third child, an older daughter, was not with them because she refused to go to church anymore.

Martha, the wife, began speaking first. "Doug, you've never met us before, but we used to pastor within twenty miles of here. In fact, we're here today because we want to apologize for the negative attitudes that we've expressed toward you over the years."

"Of course, you're forgiven. There's probably quite a bit about me to criticize, so it's all right," I smiled. "How can I help you?"

Fred spoke up. "Doug, I've heard that you understand how depression can affect leaders in ministry," he said. "I only wish I had come to speak with you sooner, because my struggle with depression has gotten me thrown out of my church."

"What? You were thrown out of your church because you lost your emotional bearings?" I asked.

"Well," Fred explained, "the church leaders said I was too depressed all the time and that my messages were always gloomy. They concluded I must not have a strong walk with the Lord, and they said they couldn't grow with a pastor like me. They fired me within two days of the first meeting about my depressed state. They didn't offer any help except to give advice on how I could improve my spiritual life."

"Would you like me to go and meet with the leaders and the congregation? Maybe we can bring some understanding to them," I offered.

He shook his head. "I'm so wounded, I just don't think I could trust that church or any church again," he said. "You know, I have given my whole life serving churches. After fifteen years of service, to reach out for help and not get it—well, it's just a bitter blow."

I suggested that Fred make an appointment with a medical doctor and a local psychiatrist to see what was causing his depression. I got word back a few weeks later that, in fact, his thyroid gland was acting irregularly, and he simply needed medication to make sure the imbalance didn't cause emotional drops.

Imagine that. A malfunctioning thyroid gland was made into a big spiritual issue resulting in a pastor's dismissal and a family's disillusionment!

I encouraged Fred to write a letter to the church—not in retribution, but simply to instruct them so that they could deal better with similar issues in the future.

No healing can occur when people who should be supporting a healing environment actually become obstacles to healing, either through ignorance or misguided notions.

A Tragic Attempt at Exorcism

Sid and Janet were in our church for about a year before they let anyone get near them. They had been members of a radical fundamentalist church that had moved into some questionable and excessive practices labeled "spiritual" by the leaders—but which were laden with spiritual and emotional abuse.

The group eventually became a full-blown cult and fell apart. It's not very often that we stop and assess the destruction caused by these kinds of situations. In Janet's case, the abuse was devastating.

One of the group's leaders had noted that Janet was excessively fearful. Besides being afraid to go on ladies' retreats and other trips, she was overly concerned about the safety of her kids and frequently asked church members to pray for her. Rather than help Janet address her fears, this leader decided she needed to have demons cast out of her.

I remember well the day she told me her story. My heart sank. I was sickened by the spiritual abuse we are all capable of.

"One Sunday night I went to church while Sid stayed home with the kids. That was the night the leader felt I should be set free of my fear," she explained in a quiet voice. "He had me sit in a chair, and he and a team of several others gathered around me and began yelling in my face, screaming at the devil. I was scared to death. I wanted them to stop, but I felt I had to do what I was told."

"You know," I said gently, "true healing never requires giving one's will over to would-be healers."

"I didn't know any better," she said. "That was the only church I had ever gone to. I figured I must be very evil to need that kind of treatment. I still can't get the picture of them screaming over me out of my mind. All I wanted to do was to get out of there!

"Eventually they gave up, and the leader said I clearly had no love for Christ in me at all. How else could the enemy have such a hold? He seemed quite angry that they weren't successful at my expense."

I didn't respond quickly. Deep spiritual wounds of this kind are very, very tender. "Have you been able to get over the fear of church authority since then?"

"No. To be very honest with you, at this point I can't bring myself to trust you or any pastor. And now that I've said that, I fear I won't be welcome here."

"Of course you're welcome here," I said. "Do you love Jesus Christ?"

"Yes."

"Well, he's the boss here," I assured her. "I care for you, and I'll do my best to watch out for you. But you may never trust me fully. That's okay. Just trust God. Trust him to work in your life."

I encouraged Janet and Sid to become part of one of our church's small groups. "I find that a small group can be a terrific place to begin recovering from pain," I explained. "And it's critical that you begin to move beyond that pain, when your heart and soul are ready."

Like Fred, our pastor friend, Janet had been part of a congregation that may have started out right but eventually moved in a wrong direction. Healing stopped. Destruction began.

Most of our churches won't have experiences quite like these, but I'll guarantee you the seeds are resident in all of them. Janet was not an object of love and compassion for that team of screamers. She was a means to authenticate their ministry. When she didn't respond the way they thought she should, they were embarrassed; they considered it a reflection on them.

We must ask ourselves: Does anyone embarrass us? We may not keep a person up all night trying to do a needless exorcism. But maybe there is someone whose lack of progress in the Lord is a thorn in our side. Their continual problems make our ministry look powerless. When we use others to prove our worth and do "marketing" for us, we're in trouble.

Hide and Seek

I've encountered many people who've felt they've had to hide in church, certain that if they were found out, they would be isolated and treated as freaks or worse.

Safety! It's one of the most important words in healing. We ought to feel safe in church, but too often, we're not. A worker in a Seattle ministry for homosexuals told me that almost three-fourths of the men they've helped were raised in strict, fundamentalist homes. Mix together a distant father, a lack of acceptance, and a distorted spirituality that makes asking for help seem like a fate worse than death; who wouldn't have struggles?

Who are the hiders? It could be the elder who knows full well that his drinking is destroying his home, yet he fears he won't be accepted if he admits a problem. Or the Sunday-school teacher who doesn't want the church to know that her husband hits her.

Or the pastor who is certain he knows how his board will react if he tells them his daughter is pregnant. Too many of us hide because our churches are harsh spiritual environments rather than havens of healing.

The son of a pastor I know was arrested for smoking marijuana on the church parking lot. It took one week for the news to spread through the church. Understand, this pastor was a good man and an effective minister. Anyone who believes that good parents can't have children who go wrong needs to be introduced to the real world.

Two weeks after the embarrassing arrest, a board meeting was called and the pastor was unceremoniously fired. He was not even allowed to say good-bye to the congregation. Now, several years later, the son is in even bigger trouble, and the whole family is a bit jaundiced about those they once sought to love and lead.

No wonder pastors hide sins! I believe denominational officials should be ashamed in situations like this for not risking to bring justice. Clearly, there is something wrong with board members who cut off a pastor this way. God must grieve!

What should the board have done? Well, how about giving the pastor two months off with pay to spend time with his family? No doubt he had put in eighty hours a week for several years, to his family's detriment. And how about repenting to the boy for asking far more from his dad than God did? How about promising the family that the church will no longer compete for their husband and father's time? Maybe a big hug would have been nice too.

Such situations create a ripple of dismay and bitterness that destroys the very thing we are seeking to build. The fact is, unless people who wreck their lives feel that they will be treated rationally and lovingly by the church, they will continue to hide. We all do it. And hiding compounds our problems.

I have concluded: Give a group of humans a stressful and embarrassing situation, and nine times out of ten we will come up with an extremely creative, stupid way of handling it. That is why I am writing this book. My eyes tear up as I think about good people who've destroyed other good people just because we in the church never talk about what to do when leaders are the ones who need healing.

I was taught in Bible school that you should never let any of your faults be known to a church, because the deacon board and the key givers in the church would not stand for it, and you would be thrown out! I decided to buck that system several years ago when I revealed my own bipolar illness to my congregation.

I don't come close to the movie stereotype of a manic-depressive person. Neither do most bipolar folks. The reactions I have faced have been painful. But I regret nothing.

Perhaps my example will help Christians face up to some of the silly notions we have about people and leaders in particular, and we'll learn to heal rather than hurt. Perhaps we'll come to understand and respect the fact that the best healers are often wounded healers.

Churches that heal will strive to be trustworthy, to create an environment of compassion, trust, and acceptance that says, "You're safe here. Let's get you healed."

Only in such an environment will we come out from our hiding places and deal honestly with our struggles.

Unfortunately, many traits work against a church's becoming a healing environment, such as:

- a belief that Christianity is primarily doing—that at the core of Christian faith is more concern about outward behavior than inner transformation
- an unwillingness to grant a healthy anonymity to those who are in great pain
- an unwillingness to network with others (such as medical doctors, twelve-step groups, and reputable community organizations) to make sure hurting people get the help they need
- a belief that the mission of the church is to make Christians perfect rather than to keep us moving forward on the road of life in Christ (We are all pilgrims on this journey, not arrivals.)
- a tendency to meddle in homes rather than simply being available to serve
- dishonesty and unwillingness on the part of leaders to be open about their own shortcomings and failures
- the use of guilt as a motivator

- excess church debt, which gives money, more than people, the upper hand in church decision-making
- the discouragement or prohibition of women from positions of leadership
- the overscheduling of meetings, keeping families from spending the time together they need to be healthy
- an unwillingness to put a stop to backbiting and gossip
- a tendency to major on minors—for example, abortion, politics, tongues, deliverance—while forgetting Bible training and the key issues of love, joy, and peace
- a lack of a representative council or board to help with major decisions
- immorality among leaders and an unwillingness to confront immorality
- a tendency to remain isolated from other churches in town

These traits encourage hiding. They say, "You're not really safe here." Of course, all churches will see something of themselves in one or more of these characteristics. No church is perfect. But churches that heal strive for integrity, and they practice acceptance. I mean just that: They *practice*. It is so foreign to us that years of practice are necessary.

Acceptance is refusing to be the lord over others. That was Jesus' point when he told the crowd standing around the adulterous woman that the most righteous one among them should cast the first stone (see John 8:3–11). The near-tragedy showed the danger of a group of people lording their "superiority" over a hurting person. It was an object lesson in the meaning of acceptance.

A HAPPY ENDING

Jerry is a pastor who leads a congregation of moderate size. In high school and college, he had been quite a drinker. Then he received Christ and stayed free of alcohol for a long time. One ill-fated day he made a terrible error. He began to drink privately to ward off the stress of ministry.

At first he thought this was fine and told himself God didn't mind. But then he realized he was having to sneak around to get his alcohol. Eventually he became less and less careful about where and how he drank. His wife became suspicious of his erratic behavior and late nights.

At church, people began to notice that he was often irritable, and his sermons were frequently ill-prepared. He had always been gregarious but now seemed to avoid contact with the congregation. Finally, several staff members began to notice the smell of liquor on his breath by midmorning.

Jerry pulled me aside after one of our pastoral prayer meetings in the city. He knew I had an interest in twelve-step groups, so he told me his story.

"What did your church do when they realized you had a problem?" I asked.

"All of my elders got together and lovingly confronted me with my wife," he said. "There was so much love in the room, so much acceptance, that I had to admit to it and respond."

"And you're still pastoring there?" I asked with a chuckle.

"Yes, that's the best part," he smiled. "Fortunately we had a strong leader in our church who is a doctor, and he influenced the rest of the group. He explained to them that alcoholism is a disease that decimates both body and spirit, and that in spite of my terrible move toward liquor, it could be cured. He pointed out that I had stood by all of them at various times in the past, and now I needed them to stand by me."

"That's incredible. How did that affect you?"

His eyes began to tear up. "I knew right then, Doug, that everything I had spoken about, everything I had taught, everything I had professed, was true. My *church healed their pastor.*"

May every pastor—may every Christian—find such a healing place.

Whether I fly with angels, fall with dust,
Thy hand made both, and I am there:
Thy power and love, my love and trust
Make one place ev'rywhere.

———— ■ ————

George Herbert, "The Temple"

3

Creating a Healing Environment

Sometimes I dream when I drive down the road—which can make for an exciting ride if you're my passenger! I had one of those dreams recently on a street not far from home. I was remembering my experience of working in an apple-juice factory during my summer and winter breaks in college.

One year, the company made me guru of the juice cans. Truckers would come and unload pallet after pallet of tin cans onto a conveyor belt. I pushed a button, and the cans would move up the belt and situate themselves, ready to be filled with high-quality juice.

Another year, I got the job of climate-control specialist. This entailed making sure that the apple storage room was kept at the perfect temperature so the apples wouldn't turn mushy before they were pressed. If the temperature wasn't just right, the apples ended up with a chemistry and consistency poor for making juice. (I will tell you a little trade secret: Apple juice is really part pear juice too. They didn't take such pains with the pears though; they stayed out in the rough climate.)

Someone had to be in charge of climate control because trucks went in and out all day, and the perfect climate was in danger if the doors were left open. They needed a dependable person to close those doors! Yep, that's right, I was a glorified doorman, but "climate-control specialist" sounds better.

My bosses were quite touchy about keeping the factory temperature just right, and they could tell if I was falling down on the job by tasting the juice that came out at the other end. So I worked hard.

My climate-control experience turned out to be useful when I became the leader of a church more than twenty years ago. Our church started out very small—just ten people in my living room. We grew to three hundred, then determined that we would really focus on evangelism. Some people didn't like that idea and left, but before too long our numbers began to explode into the thousands as more and more people met Christ through our efforts.

I soon discovered that climate control was my main job. In fact, the stress and strain of that job sometimes made me want to quit. But I'm convinced that nothing can happen in the healing realm in a church without someone being in charge of climate control.

Environment matters. It has been documented repeatedly that a strong "high-touch" environment—that is, one that offers very human benefits like friendship, encouragement, and a sense of community—enhances the immune system. Maintaining good communication in marriage and resolving work-related conflicts, for example, are proven ways to enhance immunity. In infants, a high-touch environment even decreases the mortality rate! Clearly, total health can be optimized by a good home, work, and life environment. On the other hand, an environment that lacks the positive qualities of "high-touch" will have difficulty being a healing place.

For years I spoke regularly with our church leaders about the climate of the church. I could tell when it was off balance. I remember a time in the eighties when I returned from a vacation and knew something was not right as soon as I stepped to the platform. Faces were sour and sad. *What has happened to the church?* I wondered to myself. As it turned out, a young woman who was divorcing one of our church leaders had persuaded many in the congregation that I was covering up her husband's abuse of her and her children. I knew of neither. But her rumor had affected the environment.

Climate is not something you can measure scientifically, but you can observe it, and it will show up in the statistics eventually.

In fact, God used my understanding of climate control to help me know when it was time for me to leave my pastorate. For some time, one of the things that continued to evade me was how to develop the kind of environment the Lord wanted for the church at that point in our history. As I continued to trust him and seek his guidance, it became clear that it was time for a change—both for the church and for me personally.

Now that I'm in the evangelistic and consulting fields working with a large number of churches, I'm more convinced than ever that there is an environment that releases healing. The question is: What does it look like and how do you get it?

There's No Place like Home

I travel a good deal, and it's always wonderful to return home, particularly after a long trip. I walk into my house, recognize the sounds and smells, and think, *Now, this is where I want to be*. I throw my shoes off and call, "Here I am, baby!" Instantly, I have that "at-home" feeling.

I've sensed that feeling in other places too—like the home of a couple who've been my friends for nearly thirty years. They helped found my first church. When I go to their house, their kids treat me as though I belong there, and I feel totally comfortable. There's an attitude of acceptance and a meeting of the hearts that takes place when we just glance at one another.

God has the desire for that at-home feeling as well. I think a healing environment makes God feel at home. He walks in, hears the familiar sounds, smells the familiar smells, kicks off his shoes, and says, "Here I am. Worship me!" Attaining and maintaining that at-home environment for God is essential to the task of becoming a church that heals.

The Bible actually has a great deal to say about the kind of home God likes and what happens when he fills that home. When the Old Testament refers to the "Shekinah glory" of the Lord, it's talking about the experience of God's presence coming into a place and upon his people, transforming toxic environments into health-filled ones by the power of his grace.

How important is a good "home environment" to God? Well, consider Jesus, who was a pretty successful guy early in his career. Everybody followed him. Within a matter of months, he had amassed a sort of entourage that went with him everywhere. They fetched his food, helped him move through crowds, and watched him do amazing miracles.

Then he headed toward his hometown of Nazareth. The disciples were so certain Jesus would wow the home crowd that they already had the headline picked out: Local Boy Makes Good. They were hopeful that Jesus was going to station himself in Nazareth and stop all the wandering around. (They didn't know he had already chosen Capernaum as his headquarters.)

But except for healing a few people, the Bible says Jesus didn't do any miracles there (see Mark 6:1–6). Rather, it says that he was amazed at the lack of faith in the town of his origin. In Nazareth, he determined, the environment was not conducive to healing.

"I want an environment of faith to have churches that heal," he still says today.

Is it the pastor's fault if a church does not heal? Personally, I think the pastor's role is overstated. One of the great mistakes the church has made in the last part of this century is to place an excessive amount of importance on the role of pastor. The pastor can preach great sermons and oversee the leading of great worship. He can keep a check on the climate and offer leadership when change is needed. But if the congregation itself is not creating a healthy environment—if believers are not seeking health for themselves and promoting healing for others—the toxic environment mitigates against all the sermons a pastor can preach.

So what can each of us do to add to the healing environment of our church?

First, we must be willing to take responsibility. I have gone through the agony of admitting that I was a big factor in developing an unhealthy environment in my own church at one point. But I set out to improve the climate by facing my shortcomings and getting the help I needed.

Second, we must be willing to work one act of love at a time. I think we forget that healing, ultimately, is about people and that success is measured one person at a time. We should be happy with any progress we see and give thanks.

Finally, we must pursue God above all. Every church or group has its own chemistry. The addition of people who are healthy, who pursue God honestly and with their whole heart, creates a positive chemistry in the group. On the other hand, the addition of people who have no intention of being obedient to God, who are careless in their concern for others, breeds its own negative influences.

It is important for us to remember that this is God's show. By pursuing him, we do more than just solve problems; we bring them near to God. And his presence heals.

Can a Church Change Its Environment?

The biblical view of the nature of man is that man is fluid; we change. Because of God's grace and Christ's coming to redeem us, our state can change at any moment, before and after we become Christians. I believe this works for churches too. A church can be transformed from a toxic environment to a healthy one, without switching leaders or booting people out of the church (the method tried all too often).

Change, of course, does not come easily. And it is particularly hard to turn around an entire church at once. That's why I usually recommend that churches break into small groups to discuss the issues at hand. In small groups, we benefit from hearing many perspectives, and we emphasize the importance of each individual believer's participation in the church. Individual groups must avoid the temptation, however, to look for a scapegoat or culprit for every problem. After all, all of us have a more than sufficient amount of toxicity to keep us humble.

Basically, change in any church requires three factors to be in place.

1. The desire to change—A leader can nurture a church's desire to change by emphasizing the benefits of that change. "Ought to's" are out. The desire to change has to do with the conglomerate will of the church reaching the place where it says, "I want to." In the biblical parable of the prodigal son, we see clearly that it doesn't take a lot of "want to" on the part of a sincere seeker for Christ to act.

2. *The energy within the group to change*—When it comes to change, hope is the fuse; faith is the explosion. But energy in a congregation or an individual believer—the inner capacity to hope and believe—is a nebulous thing. It is almost impossible to measure in a tangible way. Many churches have had all their energy zapped from dealing with past problems. An administrator who steals money, a pastor who has an affair, an unchecked group of gossipers—all these things can wear down a church.

Trying to resolve past issues is often necessary for closure, but we should never expect that problems will always come to a tidy conclusion. Resolution, if possible, is good, but it is not enough to repower the hope-and-faith energy needed to effect change.

I recommend that pastors start the process of rebuilding hope with a positive, future-friendly preaching plan over a period of time—sermons that emphasize the never-ending love of God and his readiness to meet us where we are. A good missions outreach or a creative project to care for the poor can help too, pointing people away from themselves and toward the very heart of God. Hope and faith grow as we see lives changed by his grace.

3. A *plan to change*—We all want instant change. But I think a plan to change anything about a church works best if it is at least two years in development. Particularly with baby boomers, planning requires a great deal of participatory involvement in order for everyone to take ownership of the change process.

Any plan must factor in a healthy perspective of progress; otherwise, discouragement can set in when things don't happen according to schedule. We Americans tend to think only in terms of "full" or "empty," "sick" or "well." But it has been my experience that most churches don't fit in an either/or category. We deal with degrees of health, rather than total health or total illness. All congregations, because of the ebb and flow of diverse humanity passing through their midst, are a mixture at best.

The goal of a healing church is to maintain an environment that is mixed stronger toward the healthy-and-whole side than the broken-and-sick side. If we do that, we're making progress.

I learned this the hard way. I pastored a magnificent outreach church. We led many hundreds of people to decisions for Christ every year. We implemented twelve-step groups before twelve-step groups were popular. Consequently, we attracted a lot of very broken people who began their healing process with us.

Over time, we found that we could not sustain a significant imbalance of, for example, too many people dealing with aberrant sexual issues in their life or too many folks wounded by dysfunctional churches. At several points, we had to take steps to slow down the growth of our congregation to keep from blowing up ourselves. And we had to be very deliberate about putting only mature, tested Christians in places of leadership or influence. A church can only help heal as many people as the strength of its core allows at any given time.

Every pastor hates to hear about people who came to their church for healing, trusting in God's community to help them repair their broken lives, only to have their expectations go unmet. I've always been particularly vulnerable to this kind of critique. It tears me up. I know that people's expectations are usually far beyond even what God will do. But it's tough when you realize you could and should have done better.

The church I led experienced many years of nearly 100 percent growth. It was a wonderful, exciting time! But a consultant friend told me we were going to pay for it eventually, and he was right. Our leadership went through a very difficult period of burnout.

Let me take you to my living room in the late eighties:

"Stella, what kind of responses have we been getting from parents about the Christian education program?"

Stella, one of our church leaders, answered, "Well, Pastor, we've gotten mostly good comments. I've sent random interview sheets out to the parents, and the responses have been very positive."

"Yes, I saw those, and they were very good," I interrupted. "But I also noticed that a lot of people are frustrated with not being fed, with not feeling a part of things. I'm curious about where we're missing it."

Les, another leader, piped up. "I think we're growing too fast, Doug."

"Yes, I think that's true," my wife, Deb, added. "I mean, just look at you guys. You look terrible!" she laughed.

Another man, John, responded with his usual coy smile that meant he'd figured out something the rest of us hadn't. "Have you noticed how the statistics in our twelve-step Lifeline programs have jumped up?" he asked. "And do any of us have a stack of phone messages to be returned that's less than three inches thick? I think we've extended ourselves beyond what we're equipped to minister to, and we'd better be careful, because we're creating expectations we can never meet."

After some discussion, we concluded that we needed to close the Lifeline programs to new people for a while until we could train another core group of leaders. It was a hard step to take, but it was necessary for the long-term benefit of everyone concerned, including those who would come to us for ministry.

Good climate controllers watch out for the strength of the core of the church. They keep their finger on the pulse of the congregation's commitment level; if large numbers are without a true commitment to the group, the church will die or burst. And they notice whether those who get healed turn around and share healing with others. If healing is hoarded, the church is in trouble.

As we discovered in our church, making an accurate assessment isn't always easy. It requires access to good, relevant, statistical information; a leadership team working together specifically to assess such things; and the intuition of the pastor. (Yes, we may as well admit it: Most effective leaders lead more by intuition than studied data.)

I have seen many well-meaning congregations like my own set out to heal people, only to find themselves off course, consumed with the task of putting out fires, and unable to recruit enough workers to care for the broken people who come in.

It must be made clear that no healing environment is possible if only the pastor carries the burden to heal. Significant numbers of volunteer lay pastors are needed to foster a healing environment. With the collapse of society's postmodern way of thinking, American Christians have a wonderful opportunity to be ministers of true healing in Christ; but only if churches, both large and small, have bivocational pastors and lay leaders to handle the care needs.

As we noted, most churches are a mixture; healing churches try to lean more toward health. How do you adjust the balance when the scales are tipping to the toxic side? One of the ways I've learned is to do what Jesus did: Raise the stakes. If growing numbers of people aren't contributing and entering into the spirit of giving, they are not well. So preach messages on giving. You may reduce the crowd, but you'll also build the core.

If your care or twelve-step programs are bringing in an influx of persons who have severe problems beyond what you can handle, simply limit the class attendance for a period of, say, six months. The numbers will stabilize, and the people who remain will get the support they need to grow into wholeness and become ministers themselves.

The Cost of Becoming a Healing Church

I won't kid you. There are costs to maintaining an environment that heals. Let's examine some of the real costs that a church will want to consider with explicit honesty before setting out to become a healing environment.

Churches that heal may have to overstep some people's comfort zones. People today look at church as one more consumer entity, choosing their congregation based on its ability to meet their needs and offer the programs they want. Churches, in response, put all their time and effort into programs that will keep everyone happy.

Clearly, America's consumer values and ethics have slipped deeply into the church, maybe never to be extracted without a dynamic exorcism of some sort!

But the fact is, a consumer cannot be a disciple. And when you're dealing with hurting people, you may need to do things or emphasize things that aren't palatable to those who are mainly interested in being kept comfortable and entertained.

Churches that heal may have to change their budget priorities. Such churches quickly discover that a significant amount of money must be spent on training healers and on helping those who are in the process of healing deal with living expenses. Most of the alcoholics and drug addicts we've worked with also struggled with tremendous financial distress. Helping them with daily expenses for a time went a long way toward supporting the healing that was taking place in their hearts.

The budget pressure can be severe. The fact is, when a church is focused on healing and outreach, a significant portion of the congregation is not able to carry its own weight financially. Staying solvent requires a lot of nerve, faith, and good budgeting.

Churches that heal may see the "quality" of their worship drop off. Of course, "quality" to God and "quality" to man are two different things. But influxes of new people in the process of healing can affect the quality or technical excellence of worship; after all, they don't know the songs; they haven't learned the routines; they don't talk the talk. They may even dress funny. It can look at times as though the congregation has "dropped down" a class or two.

Healing the hurting and wounded will require a loss of pride and a willingness to pay the price of making room.

I'm convinced God has placed at least one person in every church to embarrass the rest of us and teach us how much he loves the unlovely. We had one elderly individual in our church who was excessively friendly. He also didn't smell very clean. He couldn't contain himself from greeting nearly everybody in the church.

Several leaders said, "Can't we do something about this guy?" But I felt in my heart that the old man was a "gut check" for anyone who came into the church. Occasionally we cautioned him about being overly exuberant, but he clearly loved the church. You know, our congregation grew to love him and not mind him at all, though he did certainly break our pride on numerous occasions.

Churches that heal will attract problem people. A church that becomes known as a place that helps people get healed in a disciplined yet compassionate way will soon find large numbers of hurting and broken individuals hanging around! Some of these people, if not yet fully committed to Christ and a godly healing process, may even be dangerous. A church's staff and leaders must be trained to spot predatory or menacing behavior at all levels.

The threat of physical danger can be real. For example, if a wife and husband are both cocaine addicts, and the wife—as I have seen over and over again—chooses to come to Christ and walk away from drugs, the husband in his addictive rage may become a danger to everyone. We had an attempted arson on our building because of such a circumstance.

Churches that heal can burn out their pastoral leaders and volunteers. At one point, our church was experiencing a high level of staff turnover. I assumed the problem was that I was a terrible manager until I had a consultant come in and put his finger on it. After looking at the large number of decisions for Christ we were having each week and seeing the high number of outreach and care programs we maintained for wounded people, he concluded, "Your calling has gotten away from you. You should only try to do what is healthy and reasonable for each one of you. And at the end of the day, Jesus will have to cover the rest." These words were both comforting and challenging. Burnout is truly a risk of churches that seek to be healing entities.

BEFORE YOU BEGIN

If, after considering the cost, you decide to become a healing church, here are seven clear steps to take:

1. *Analyze the current healing capacity of your church*. That capacity can be discovered by knowing certain numbers: the percentage of people who have sound Bible knowledge, the percentage of regular givers, the percentage of people who share their spiritual gifts, etc.

2. *Assess the ability of your core leaders and volunteers to handle more care*. If the church has a large number of mature, healthy people, the opportunities are great. However, if there is not a strong core of people who've moved on from their beginning points in Christ to greater healing and wholeness, you'll need to find ways to invest in that maturing process before seeking to heal further.

3. *Save up the money*. Try to set aside enough to have maybe 5 to 10 percent of your budget put into support and care for those who need to be healed.

4. *Develop the desire and energy for change within your group*. Sometimes that involves stoking the fires of dissatisfaction with the status quo. Visit some healing churches and observe some of the great healing victories taking place in other congregations, then discuss how your own church can experience the same thing. Present a clear vision of your church as a healing entity in your community.

5. *Get the word out through small focus groups*. I've found that large meetings are poor vehicles for introducing new

ministry concepts, recommending changes, or soliciting insight. Have the small groups begin to discuss the kinds of broken people that may exist within the immediate five miles around your church.

6. *Establish a "start date."* This will set you on your journey with intercessory prayer, celebration, and rejoicing.
7. *Celebrate!* Celebrate those who come to Christ. Celebrate the decisions of believers to step out in ministry and become part of your church's healing core.

As pastors and leaders, we are doing something far more complex than making apple juice, I know. But there is a lesson to be learned from my experience as a college-age climate-control specialist: We must never get so caught up with the task of getting the apples on the conveyor belt that we forget about the quality of the juice coming out on the other side. Only by keeping a close watch on the climate in our congregations will we be able to maintain the kind of spiritual environment that is necessary to be churches that heal.

See, I will send you the prophet Elijah before that great and dreadful day of the LORD *comes. He will turn the hearts of the fathers to their children, and the hearts of the children to their fathers; or else I will come and strike the land with a curse.*

Malachi 4:5–6

4

Contending for the Extended Family

For the vast majority of people, life development takes place in the context of a family—although admittedly, in this day and age, what that family looks like and who it consists of may vary considerably. Whether it's a good family or a bad family, a strong family or a weak family, a healthy family or a toxic family makes a big difference for the children growing up within it. The first six years of any child's life, experts say, are a great determiner of what will occur over the sixty or seventy years that follow. In other words, who we are is pretty much set by the time we're in grade school, and our families have been the biggest influence!

As a church leader interested in healing, I've asked myself: *What if families viewed themselves as the primary healing zone of the church?* After all, it seems to me that since the sixties we've let the organized church take a role similar to the state. Overreliance on the paid church staff and church programs has caused us to get lazy about how we operate as families. When I first became a pastor, I remember being shocked at how many families let the church feed their relatives instead of doing it themselves.

Most healing, even in later life, takes us back to our families in one way or another. I've counseled men who've been married twenty or thirty years yet still react to women based upon their childhood experience with an excessively dominating mother. I've prayed with asthma suffers whose allergic manifestations become worse while discussing an absentee father or cruel grandfather. The pathway to healing definitely goes through the family secrets we all carry.

Considering this, I can't help but wonder: Is the church stepping in where it shouldn't? Are we taking away from families what is theirs to do rather than equipping them to nurture and heal at home?

I'm convinced that healthy families can provide needed preventative medicine for what ails us. In a world caught up in the tidal wave of the Fall, good ethical and moral development in the home—plus a family's love and healthy physical touch—can promote health and healing. Churches that heal will choose to major on equipping families to be the healthy centers of spiritual life.

THE IMPORTANCE OF THE FAMILY

Not long ago, a story hit the national news about a boy who had been terrorizing his neighborhood by breaking into houses and taking little goodies for himself. He was caught, but rather than charging the kid with delinquency, the court charged his mother for failing to control him!

Holding parents accountable for their children...what a concept! It seems to fly in the face of our modern society's "victim mentality," as well as recent liberal policies that give more say-so to government than to parents in areas such as their children's education. But a shift is occurring, and I'm happy to see it. At least in some courts of law, the family is being recognized as the God-given center of moral and physical healing.

That's a biblical position. In John 2, we see Christ's commitment to the centrality of the Jewish home in Israel. Jesus had just begun his messianic unveiling. It was an important time, yet he stopped to heed his mother's request to attend a wedding in Cana, bringing his disciples with him. It was undoubtedly the wedding of a family member; you would never bring friends from out of town to the wedding of a family you didn't feel comfortable imposing upon! But Jesus knew family celebrations were important, and he demonstrated that.

Later Acts 10 tells us about the conversion of a Roman centurion's family. The apostle Peter was stunned when Cornelius's entire household turned to Christ. This was the first entry of the gospel into a purely Gentile realm, and it was no coincidence that a family was at the center. The family is the primary springboard for spiritual growth and the ultimate of healings—the healing of our sinfulness through faith in Christ. On that day, Cornelius's whole family was baptized in water, baptized into the Holy Spirit, and committed fully to Christ's kingdom, as only the Jews had experienced up to that point.

Paul also expressed his commitment to the family's central role in his first letter to the young evangelist Timothy. He cautioned Timothy not to be too quick to allow the church to take the place of the family: "Give proper recognition to those widows who are really in need. But if a widow has children or grandchildren, these should learn first of all to put their religion into practice by caring for their own family and so repaying their parents and grandparents, for this is pleasing to God....If anyone does not provide for his relatives, and especially for his immediate family, he has denied the faith and is worse than an unbeliever" (1 Timothy 5:3–4, 8).

The benevolence program of the early church was a sort of welfare system for widows who had no family to help support them. It was not available to widows who had sons or daughters or even grandchildren. What a challenge this is to us today!

I have estimated from my discussions with different pastors that of all the resources churches extend toward people who request help, as much as one-third is being spent unbiblically. Rarely is the question asked: Have you pursued your family's help first?

The family, I believe, must be our first line of spiritual defense. If you wonder where you own church stands on this, ask yourself:

- Do you regularly encourage adult children and grandchildren to take responsibility for their elders?
- Is your church too willing to take on the bulk of the responsibility for the spiritual development of children? Do you have a program for training parents to teach their own kids?
- Have you ever required the restoration of a person to their family before offering benevolence?

THE SABBATH DINNER

I'm a member of the board of a wonderful organization called the International Fellowship of Christians and Jews, directed by my good and trusted friend, Rabbi Yechiel Eckstein. Yechiel has taught me many things about the Bible and about the Jewish origins of Christianity. I've come to believe that we Christians would do well to go back to the Jewish roots of our faith and draw from that deep well, particularly as it relates to the spiritual disciplines of the family.

A key tradition in Jewish families is the keeping of the Sabbath—children, parents, and grandparents together, remembering and worshiping God. Today's church promotes the exact opposite. We're so dichotomized that kids go to one classroom, teenagers to another. Seniors go to the early service, baby boomers to the late one. We rarely get our people together on a family level for worship.

I was bold last year and asked Yechiel if Deb and I could come to his home and attend a Shabbat evening with his family. He graciously agreed.

It was fascinating to watch as the Sabbath meal was passed around the table, scriptures were read, songs were sung, and children responded to their father's questions about the Lord.

I love the way orthodox fathers train their children in the Word of God. It is not deductive. By this I mean they don't say, "Here are three things Moses said. Memorize them." Rather, it is inductive. It is a learning style based on asking open-ended questions or making false statements that the children then correct.

In our meal that evening, Yechiel referred to a passage from the Law and asked a question about Abraham that led to a discussion about the grace of God. I realized he was showing me how his family learns, and he was showing me that his Jewish faith, too, has an understanding of grace.

What caught my attention most, however, was the seriousness with which this orthodox Jewish father approached his responsibility to train his children in spirituality.

It makes me wonder: If Christian fathers and mothers, whether in two-parent or single-parent families, trained their children in the Scriptures on a regular basis and celebrated their faith in God over a weekly meal together, what would worship in our churches be like?

What if believers came to meetings not so much to get as to give unto God and respond to him out of joyful hearts cultivated in their own homes? What if the fundamental training in the Word and Christian living happened first in the families? How would our churches be different?

I make my friends nervous with the way I twiddle and tamper with some of the sacrosanct facets of church life. Of course, this is going into print, so you can see how careful I am not! But for years I've thought churches might be better off spending Christian education time and resources on training fathers and mothers, giving them the skills and tools they need to train their own children in the Bible at home. Wouldn't that make more sense then expecting kids to grow up in Christ by spending an hour a week in a Sunday-school class with one teacher responsible for ten or twenty students?

Could it be that the way we do Sunday school usurps the primacy of the role of the head of the family?

REPAIRING THE BREACHES

Malachi prophesied that one of the signs of an awakened land would be that the children's hearts would be turned to their fathers (see Malachi 4:6). In other words, breaches in the family structure would be restored by God's Spirit and power.

Good relationships with our nuclear and extended families are essential to healing and wholeness. Yet it is the rare individual who has most or all of his extended family in the near vicinity of thirty miles. What a tremendous loss!

My memories of my grandparents are some of my dearest. I had the privilege of introducing my grandmother to the Lord Jesus Christ.

It was the first sermon I preached. When she came forward, I thought it was to encourage me for doing a good job.

I spoke to her for a moment then walked away. But she didn't move, and she looked a little disappointed.

"Grandma, is there something else you wanted?" I asked.

"Yes," she answered. "I want to receive Christ, and I want to be prayed for."

At the time, she had a very bad heart, and she also had been treated for cancer. The doctors predicted she wouldn't make it much longer. But she lived ten more years, and I was able to go often to her home to talk about the Lord. We had fun, Grandma and I.

My granddad also accepted the Lord in his own inimitable way, quietly yet sincerely. I was the only one he would talk with about Christ. He loved to tell me that I was going to be a better preacher than Billy Graham.

These are rich and deep memories. I'm saddened when I meet people who don't have these kinds of experiences to remember or who've tossed them aside, not realizing the deep value that lies within them.

Of course, today's families are different from what they used to be. Many of them are "blended families" in which both husband and wife bring children from previous relationships into the home. Under one roof are her kids, his kids, and sometimes even their kids. Life, relationships, and memories can get complicated.

But blended homes can still be very loving and healthy experiences. I have known many that are. The families that commandeer the blended experience most effectively learn not only to honor diverse past experiences but also to create new experiences and memories. The church needs to give special attention to blended families, teaching them how to make their homes a spiritual center and a place of healing. Family life must be deliberate to be healthy, even in the best of homes.

A POOR FAMILY SUBSTITUTE

In the next chapter, we will talk about the importance of small groups to build a sense of "family" among believers. But in general, the church—that is, the typical Sunday corporate experience—is a poor substitute for family. Oh, we try. In fact, some of our churches have become downright codependent. They don't heal; they keep people sick by doing too much for them, by trying to be something for them that they're not supposed to be. I ask you: Should we really feel an obligation to provide a social calendar for everyone called to Christ? Should we be happy when we're the only source of fellowship for the people we lead?

I have often mused about whether the seemingly insatiable cries of some church people for more fellowship isn't a symptom of a general lackadaisical attitude toward family or a lack of emphasis on our part about the value and responsibility of the nuclear family. Maybe it's a sign of a not-so-thoughtful mind-set among believers that fails to recognize a simple fact: You'll never have another family.

The church cannot replace family. Nor can it handle family issues for its members. A weathered old leader whom I love dearly once told me, "Doug, don't take other people's problems for them. Sometimes they need to struggle with them and discover God in the answers."

One Sunday, I noticed a young man in his early thirties hanging around after one of our church services. I had just finished preaching, and a number of people had surrounded me. Once the crowd subsided, he approached.

"Can we sit down and talk?" he asked.

"Sure," I said, and motioned to the seats on the front row.

"Pastor," he confided, "I need some help from the church really bad. I'm about to lose everything I own."

"Well, I haven't seen you around here very much. How long have you been coming here?" I asked.

"About six months now," he answered, wringing his hands. I could see perspiration developing on his forehead.

"Why don't you tell me what the issue is," I said gently.

"Pastor, I have a gambling problem, and I've bet my whole next paycheck," he blurted out. "I already owe a lot of money. I'm months behind on my car. I just keep feeling I'm going to win. But I lose. I don't know what to do."

"Gambling debts," I said. "Hmm. I don't think my council will be excited about the idea of the church paying off gambling debts for you."

Then it struck me. This was a situation where the family was better suited than the church to heal this young man's life.

"Do you have a father?" I asked.

"Yes. He lives about forty miles from here. But he would never help me with this kind of thing."

"Have you and your father had a break in communication?"

The young man shook his head affirmatively.

"Does he know about your problem?"

"No."

"Well, then, here's what we're going to do," I said. "We're going to get you into some counseling, and then into Gamblers Anonymous. I'll tell you what, I'll personally pay for your first three visits to the counselor. But I also want to talk to your father on the phone, and I would like you to be there with him when I am talking to him. You, your father, and I are going to work together to help you get out of this mess. Could you arrange this?"

"Yes," he promised.

The next day the young man drove to his father's house, and I called there at the time we'd prearranged. I talked to the father about his God-given responsibility to help his son, to show tough love, and to become an avenue that God could use to work out his son's salvation and healing. Fortunately, the father was more than willing to do his part, especially since I agreed to help enforce some of the stipulations he would need to impose to help his son overcome the gambling addiction.

When we finished the conversation, his father added, "I never thought a preacher would call me up and show so much respect for me as a father! I thought you guys liked to be the whole show."

I chuckled. "Actually, the Bible says that you have the primary responsibility for developing your family spiritually," I said. "Are you a Christian, sir?"

"No," he answered. "But I want to come hear you preach."

"That's a fine start."

Churches that heal recognize that God-established pathways already exist to shape and train lives, and they don't try to usurp them. For twenty-five years, I've watched ministry leaders with the best of intentions wear themselves out trying to replace what God has already established in the family.

I feel we have a long way to go in this area. The church needs to rethink everything from benevolence care, to the training of children, to the development of leaders. I'm convinced that parents are the ones primarily responsible for developing leadership gifts in their children. The church's role is to recognize those gifts and make room for them—just as Timothy's gifts, developed by a faithful mother and grandmother, were recognized and encouraged by Paul (see 2 Timothy 1:5–6).

Connecting with Extended Families

So what can you do to help the people in your church connect with their families in a healthy, life-giving way? Following are several suggestions.

- Preach three sermons a year on the primacy of families in developing and nurturing spiritual growth.
- Four times a year, have an effective father (or mother) and son (or daughter) share their secrets to growing together spiritually. One short, anecdotal success story will do more than a litany of "thou shalts."
- Prepare a curricular approach in your Sunday school that leans heavily on the responsibility of the head of the household. Develop teams within your Christian education department that train and support not only teachers, but parents as well.
- Recommend, make available, and budget for creative tools to help heads of households share their faith creatively with their children. Excellent family videos are available, for example, covering portions of both the Old and New Testaments.
- Make it a requirement that pastoral counselors encourage people to restore their relationships with their parents,

pursuing what I call the "Malachi miracle." Many of the people I've counseled over the years, including nearly 100 percent of the drug addicts and alcoholics, have had to go back home, repent, and restore family bonds before experiencing complete healing.

- Teach regularly that the church is not meant to, and never can, replace the family. Small groups can get close, but church programs will never duplicate that wonderful, wholesome feeling of families sharing a life together.
- Share two or three messages a year on how breaking relationships with extended family members can cause spiritual damage. This will lay a foundation for honoring the extended family.
- Once a year, preach a message and have a celebration trumpeting the value of aunts and uncles, nephews and nieces, grandparents and grandchildren. Have an entire extended family share in the presentation.
- Train counselors and leaders (who are often codependent by nature) not to pick up the family problems and issues of those they are seeking to help. Tough love is necessary to restore the true source of God's healing to broken people.

WHEN FAMILIES ARE TOXIC

Even as I write this, I can hear many of you thinking: *Yes, but what about the people in my church who come from dysfunctional families? What if the only home they have is toxic?*

Let me answer this in two ways. First, if by "toxic" you mean that the family isn't Christian, then I'd encourage you to think again. I have found that the gospel is enriched in the eyes of an unbelieving family when the one who's been converted trusts God to use that family as a true source of his life and power. Respect begets respect.

However, if by "toxic" you mean that the home is filled with alcoholism, sexual abuse, or personality disorders that make it impossible for family members to connect, I agree there is a problem. And unfortunately, it is a widespread one in our world today. In such cases, there is a true need for the church to step in and provide opportunities for people to experience something that approximates the blessings of a home and family. Sometimes this can be accomplished simply by encouraging families to "adopt" someone who has nowhere to go on Christmas or Thanksgiving. A program of small groups is another way for those who are literally fatherless to settle in and find a "family."

After all, the church is the family of God, and God is our gracious, loving Father. Local churches that respect and appreciate families, large and small; that encourage the Malachi miracle by turning children's hearts toward home; and that share God's father-heart and the spirit of family with those in need—these will become known in their communities as churches that heal.

The proper office of a friend is to side with you when you are in the wrong. Nearly anybody will side with you when you are in the right.

■

Mark Twain

5

Majoring on Relationships

If you live to middle age, as I have, you collect a lot of stuff. I have two pieces of stuff that are more than stuff though.

The first is my grandfather's mason trowel. It was given to me from Granddad's estate when he died. It is a prized possession. When I look at it, I remember years and years of watching him as he'd lift that trowel and pound the mortar, first on the left, then on the right. He'd place a block on top, tapping it lightly with the butt end of this trowel, then artistically swipe both ends of the block, and repeat the process again and again.

The whole time he'd be telling me funny stories. He'd talk about the giant fish he caught a decade before or about the basketball games he won nearly single-handedly when he was a kid in Iowa. Each and every word he spoke to me exuded the richest love.

The second of my prized possessions is a quilt. Now, hold on, I'm a very masculine man, but I treasure this quilt! My grandmother made it. She gave it to me when I was in grade school—small pieces of fabric stitched together with tiny, precise strokes of the needle, carefully handcrafted, piece after piece, stitch after stitch. No matter how long

Granddad and I would work in the garden or drive around in his pickup, when we came back to the house we'd find her sitting there, hour after hour, day after day, making a new quilt for some member of our very large family.

When I came home after college, the first thing I did was visit my grandmother. There she was, preparing quilts for her three newest grandchildren for Christmas! One of my aunts was with her, helping her with things around the house and yard. Grandma had arthritis by then, and every stitch caused her to wince a bit. Her eyes weren't good, and she stuck her thumb quite often. But she just kept smiling and working, saying, "This color will fit a little boy just fine."

"Mom, we can take you down to the store, and you can buy Christmas presents for those kids," my aunt chastised. "You have no business working this hard and straining yourself."

My grandmother got quite animated at that point. "We'll not buy any gifts for any of my children or grandchildren," she insisted. "I never have, and I'm not going to start now. When I give one of these quilts, I'm not giving them a gift; I'm giving them myself. I want them to remember me. This is my labor, and they will know what it means."

Modern life makes it so easy to go buy something that ought to be given only from the heart. To this day, when I put my quilt to my face, I smell Grandma's house and see her small hands working away.

My trowel and my quilt aren't just "stuff." They're the symbols of a rich relationship. They help me understand what Paul meant when he said that three things will remain after all else is gone: faith, hope, and love (see 1 Corinthians 13:13). I am persuaded that our relationships are the only things that will go with us into the next life. As church leaders, we need to learn how to create an environment where true, deep, and loving relationships are fostered.

Churches that heal major on relationships. No doubt many of us would say off the top of our head, "Of course, our church does that." Before you make that assumption, however, ask yourself these questions:

- What do you spend the majority of your time talking about in staff meetings, board meetings, and prayer times?
- What do you spend your money on? Do you have more budgeted for a radio program or the latest technological equipment than for small groups?

There's no lack of new, cutting-edge programs and other "good things" we can spend time, energy, and money on. The question is, do they keep us from the main task of building loving, lasting relationships? Do they lead to healing, or do they distract us from it?

Programs have a way of defining success that a focus on relationships cannot. You can't measure the quality of relationships within your church based on the numbers that attend the Saturday men's breakfast or the Wednesday mothers-of-toddlers meeting.

Relationship success is essentially immeasurable. We may never know the score until we arrive in heaven.

Churches that heal make certain that every facet of their ministry is people-oriented and relationship-based. Success is defined in those intangible terms of hearts that have been bonded together as we all discover Christ together. It is measured in the growth of healthy, life-giving relationships. It is demonstrated when we become vulnerable with one another, talk about our sins together, and encourage one other toward spiritual growth—when we learn to give and receive ministry from someone other than the "big guy" in the pulpit.

To help me evaluate the relative health or toxicity of relationships in my own church, I developed the following checklist, based on traits I see modeled in the life of Jesus. In healthy relationships:

- Everyone equally gives and equally receives over time.
- Confidences are guarded.
- The Bible is central, and biblical principles are the guide.
- Forgiveness is readily extended.
- Friendship is based on loyalty, even when someone is wrong. (I've always been fascinated by the fact that Jesus called Judas "friend" before the fatal kiss was planted on his cheek.)
- Love is unconditional—not, "I'll love you if you love me" or, "I'll do this for you if you'll do that for me."
- Separation, when necessary, takes place on a positive note. When true friends part, there are tears, good-byes, and blessings. But healthy friendships don't end with an abrupt, "I don't care."
- There's more listening than talking.
- No one is superior. All parties consider themselves peers.

The Bible clearly demonstrates that relationships with family and friends were fundamental to the way Jesus carried out ministry. His first four disciples were interrelated: John and James were brothers who some scholars believe were Jesus' first cousins; Peter and Andrew were brothers and colleagues of John and James. Even John the Baptist was Jesus' first cousin.

Jesus was also close friends with Mary, Martha, and Lazarus, who were themselves a very close-knit family. And in John 11, we see the amazing release of resurrection power that took place among them.

I'm convinced that the power of any church is in the strength of its interconnecting friendships and relationships. Most churches have at least a start in this direction since the vast majority of people are brought to church in the first place by a family member or friend.

Ask yourself: Does your church have the kind of relationships that release power? Without an emphasis on relationships, a church's healing potential is greatly diminished. I wish I had learned this years ago. I thought that growing a great church had to do with offering programs that kept people involved; gradually I learned that relationships were the key. But making that paradigm shift wasn't easy. God had to do most of the work.

Small Groups That Heal

The small-group movement is popular in American churches. People get together in small groups of ten or twelve to study the Bible, pray, and socialize in a faith-based context. Also called cell or home groups, these small groups have proven to be great tools for spiritual growth, doctrinal teaching, effective ministry, and—most importantly—the development of healthy relationships. I've heard it said that any church program that doesn't produce small groups that can gather to assimilate and actualize the teaching is, in fact, a waste of time. I tend to agree.

I believe that in the church of the twenty-first century, small groups will be the fundamental point of ministry. In the not-too-distant future, the cost of large facilities will be prohibitive, and debt will be dangerous. Churches will have to meet less often and in smaller numbers. The ministry will have to embrace the nonprofessional. (Gee, this seems familiar...it's beginning to sound like the New Testament!) Churches that heal will recognize that the small group is the vanguard of all ministry, both now and in the future.

Like relationships in general, however, small groups can be healthy or toxic. I vividly remember a conversation I had once with a pastor named Lance. "I hate home groups sometimes," Lance told me.

"Why?" I asked, surprised.

"My wife and I started a group, and it was going great. In fact, we used the meeting as a model of what small groups in our church were supposed to be. We hated leaving the group," he said.

"When we knew we had to move on, we put a guy named Dale in as the leader," he continued. "Dale seemed like a great guy, but we didn't know a lot about him. It turned out that he was into risky investments.

"He and his wife got the whole group feeling sorry for them because they were struggling financially. The group prayed for them to be blessed. The very next week he showed up at the meeting saying that their prayers had been answered: A great investment opportunity had just come in.

"The end of the story is that Dale took the group for sixty thousand dollars! Now he's telling them that the investment didn't pay off and he has lost all their money. These are not wealthy people either! What would you do if you were me, Doug?"

"Well, I'd check Dale's credentials and call the police to see if he's ever defrauded anyone else," I said slowly. "Then I would go meet with the group, making sure he is present, and expose him. Obviously, this group is toxic."

"Toxic?" Lance said. "What do you mean?"

"Toxic groups are ones that poison their members rather than promote health," I explained. "They may have any number of negative traits, but they are always manipulative and hurtful toward honest people. I think about 10 percent of small groups turn toxic without close management."

We talked some more, then ended our meeting in prayer. As I left, I was glad that while toxic groups do exist, I could recall many more examples of healthy small groups than toxic ones.

I thought of Jerry, a retired pastor in our church who took over the leadership of one of our home groups. When Jill, a young single mother recovering from alcoholism and heroin addiction, began attending, Jerry laid down the law that she couldn't participate unless she agreed to be honest with the members and also join a twelve-step recovery group.

She did both. Each week the group prayed for her, but they didn't let her problems dominate the meetings.

One of Jill's biggest struggles was with finances. Jerry told the group in her presence that they were not to give her money but that she should go through the established church method which would assure that she learned accountability and budgeting. It was tough love, but it worked. Jill grew spiritually and got better and better.

At one point, Jill confided to some of the members that she was hoping to take a night course in computers so she could get a better job to support her child. Recognizing that this was a healthy step, one of the men called her parents on the East Coast. They were not well off, but they offered to send fifty dollars a month to a fund set up with our church administrator. The group members committed another four hundred dollars a month to the fund. Jill never knew it was her small group that had extended a scholarship of 450 dollars a month to make it possible for her to go to school. Not only Jill but everyone involved grew from the experience.

How can you tell the difference between healthy small groups and toxic ones? Here are some keys:

- Healthy small groups are not dominated by one person. Everyone finds a balance between communicating and listening. In toxic groups, one or two people talk, and everyone else listens.
- Healthy groups are firm in their support of one another. Toxic groups tear down and make fun of people's lives and pain.
- Healthy groups respect one another's thoughts and opinions. No "party line" is pushed; the group understands that everyone is in process, discovering how to live and grow in Christ. Toxic groups, on the other hand, show disrespect for opinions different from their own.
- Healthy groups emphasize action and living out new truths discovered in the Bible. Toxic groups spend their time in postulation and theory; their discussions are void of any presentation of the Scriptures.
- Healthy groups are trusting. That sense of trust grows as the group stays together. Toxic groups have two or three people who distrust each other, poisoning the atmosphere.
- Healthy small groups are playful and enjoy humor. Toxic groups have no time for fun; everything must be serious.

- Healthy groups foster responsibility. Every member shares responsibility for the quality of the group. Toxic groups are the responsibility of one or two people who inevitably do not meet the expectations of everyone else involved (who then feel justified to complain and gripe).
- Healthy groups respect the privacy of all participants. They don't push people faster than they want to go in their self-disclosure. Toxic groups don't respect the need for some people to open up in their own time.
- Healthy groups demonstrate a commitment to service by encouraging members to take part in serving their congregation and their community. Toxic groups consider participation in the group "service" enough.
- Healthy groups are quick to seek help when problems arise in the group. Toxic groups never seek help and tend to distance themselves from those assigned by God to bring healing, correction, and direction.

Training Leaders in the Art of Healing

Relationships within a congregation are shaped by the styles modeled by their visible and "silent" leaders. In a healthy church, leaders have the primary task not of getting things done but of maintaining a style of healthy relationships their congregation can duplicate.

Let me tell you about two leaders I've worked with. We'll call the first one Stan and the second one Ted.

Stan's solution for solving most squabbles in his area of ministry was to quit. He just couldn't stand conflict. Conflict can be healthy, however, if leaders develop good relationship skills to navigate through it. Quitting isn't one of them.

"My small-group leaders never show up for the training, and they do exactly what they want in their meetings. They don't want to take any direction from me. It's clear they'd be happiest if I quit," Stan barked at me once.

"That's not the answer," I responded. "Have you actually sat down and talked with them about this? Maybe they don't realize how important it is that we have some structure."

"No way," he said, intent on his assessment. "They just want to do their own thing because they really don't want to follow me."

"Stan," I said gently, "I want you to step back for a little bit. I have someone I want you to learn from about being a supervisor. You're not the bad guy here, and neither are the other folks. You just need to learn some healthy skills of confrontation. Good relationships aren't about no conflict; they're about honest and clear communication. As leaders, we'll have a long-term, negative impact on relationships in the church if we don't learn how to model loving, committed confrontation," I said.

Stan agreed to follow my suggestion. In fact, he learned well and became a successful leader and supervisor. As a result, the small groups under his care also learned the sound, biblical method of conflict resolution.

Ted was a different kind of leader. As a personnel manager for an aerospace company, his relationship skills were well developed. He believed in fostering an atmosphere of mutual respect. In monthly debriefing sessions, he allowed the leaders under his supervision to point out areas where he had dropped the ball. He then modeled how a person handles biblical correction.

Everyone received critiques in these sessions, but always in a spirit of love. The leaders carried this positive environment into their homes and small groups.

It takes healthy leaders to create a healthy environment. That's why leaders of small groups and other lay-ministry leaders need to be trained not just what to do but what to be. Of course, they should be taught the basics in theology and ministry. They should be encouraged to be "forever-learners," as I like to say. But beyond that, they should be taught to be sensitive, bold, and courageous in their calling, relying upon the Holy Spirit to draw from their training and knowledge of the Scriptures to address specific situations.

In the process, we shouldn't be surprised when they make mistakes. Why is it that we in the church spend so much energy trying not to make mistakes, when it is entirely obvious that we're going to make them anyway and that they're likely to be huge? For years I made the mistake of wanting everything in my church and ministry to be "perfect." Later I learned to settle for "effective." Effectiveness is usually loaded with inefficiencies and elements of mediocrity as it develops. When I was going for "perfect," I had little patience with the process.

Laypeople will never become healers if they feel they must be "perfect." Let's face it. As hard as we may try, things will never be perfect in a growing situation. They can still be conducive to healing though, if we have an attitude that says, "We're not looking for perfection; we're looking for growth."

Involving more people in ministry is important in a healing church. Some of us need to step back from our ingrained systems of church management and ask: Why do we have one couple—the pastor and his wife—doing 75 percent of the church work?

My evaluations show that in a congregation of one hundred, there are at least thirty to forty people who can do everything the paid guys do—just not as quickly or in as much volume because they work elsewhere for a living. But the load can be spread out, and when that happens, the healing dynamic is ensured. The alternative is that the thirty to forty never grow in their gifts and the pastor wears out and has a heart attack at the age of fifty-five.

A psychiatrist friend of mine surmised from his experience that pastors die twenty years younger than people in other professions. Their wives die earlier than that! He said the reason is that we never let the laypeople do what they can do at least as well as the professional people.

We must start by giving lay leaders courage and the permission to go for it. We must allow them to make mistakes. And we must train our churches to expect that a broadly delegated lay ministry is normative, not unusual.

Unfortunately, people have been trained for generations to receive ministry only from paid ministers. This unwillingness to accept ministry from laypeople and the broad unwillingness to accept ministry from women—paid or not—are perhaps the two greatest inhibitors to a true awakening of healing in the church in America. We will continue to burn out and destroy pastors and their families until we learn to humble ourselves and receive ministry from someone without a title.

In the development of lay leaders, relationships are key. I believe a system of mentoring—partnering no more than five lay leaders with one pastor or well-trained layperson—is the most effective training method for this reason. Besides, some things are better "caught" than "taught."

Furthermore, the best training is interactive—that is, it responds to the real questions people have as they actually do ministry. I'm aware of a church that requires nearly twenty training sessions before someone can teach Sunday school. Prospective teachers are discouraged before they get halfway through! No one can be expected to assimilate that much information before they start acting.

A better way is to arrange for a new person to work with a good, well-trained teacher for a few weeks, developing a relationship with that teacher so that there's a free flow of questions and answers. Such on-the-job experience ought to be simultaneous with any formal training—or even precede training. Then people know what questions to ask.

I went through college a couple of years later than my peers. I'd gotten married very young, and we'd had a son, and I'd given myself to the development of my Christian life before deciding how to proceed. I had worked hard enough and long enough and had seen enough by the time I got to college that I went through very quickly. I did most of my work in about a year and a half.

I noticed that those who studied before they'd had life experience had a tougher time. As for me, I'd already led Bible studies, small groups, and more. I wanted to assimilate all I could. I asked lots of questions because I knew what questions to ask!

How to Destroy a Healthy Environment

As we've said, healthy relationships in leadership and throughout a congregation create a church environment conducive to healing. But since the beginning of the church, a number of factors have sought to tear away at relationships and poison a healing environment.

In 1 Corinthians 11:17–19, Paul wrote: "In the following directives, I have no praise for you, for your meetings do more harm than good. In the first place, I hear that when you come together as a church, there are divisions among you, and to some extent I believe it. No doubt there have to be differences among you to show which of you have God's approval."

Apparently, Paul expected differences of opinion in the church. He even saw purpose in them. But he was not happy with the way that certain believers in Corinth were creating factions, trying to draw others into their group's way of seeing things. Earlier in his letter, he chided them for quarreling over who they were following—whether Paul, Apollos, Peter, or Christ.

Four obstacles that break down relationships in churches today include:

1. A *divisive spirit*. Any time members of a group begin talking in terms of us and them, relationships are torn down. This is not the vocabulary of Christian love. It would be hard to calculate how many churches have been divided by what the Bible calls a "party spirit." Many strong ministers simply give up from the sheer energy-drain of dealing with divisive people.

For this reason, I believe all prospective leaders—paid or lay—should be made well aware of their church's mission and vision, and their support of that vision should be assured in advance. Far too many churches make the mistake of quickly installing people into leadership who have the Christian talk down, only to discover they really weren't sold on the church's mission; they were looking for a platform for themselves. Hence, the relational fabric of the church is unraveled.

2. *Silly disagreements*. This has to be one of the enemy's favorite tactics: sparking disagreements over things that don't really mean much. If we demonstrated the spiritual fruits of patience, kindness, and the other attributes that go with love, such minor issues would melt away. But too often, we don't, and they don't.

I have a particular interest in developing worship models for specific settings, tuned to our modern times. In the area of preferred worship styles, however, I am finding that our lovelessness is catching up with us. In some congregations, the simple entrance of a drum can set up a quarrel real quickly—even a church split! The fact is, the question of traditional versus contemporary worship is the number one source of conflict in churches today.

My question is, is it really that important? Is it more important than God's love? I think not. (There is one silver lining to this cloud: We're likely to spark a barrage of new church plants over the worship issue, which will net us more churches with which to reach the lost.)

3. *Debt*. Recently, I sat in on a leadership meeting of a particular church that was trying to figure out why attendance had fallen off so drastically. Denominational leaders, church leaders, and the pastoral team were all present. Someone suggested that it was the pastor's fault; perhaps he was not healthy emotionally or spiritually. (He seemed fine to me.) Others noted the fact that two people with platform ministries had fallen morally. (*That would certainly have a profound impact*, I thought.)

The line of discussion became increasingly disrespectful, and many comments started hitting below the belt. As everyone tried to blame someone else, I leaned back in my chair and asked myself, *Where is love? Where is God's love!*

I knew everyone in the room well. They all loved the Lord, and they loved each other. They prayed together. Several had even gone through deep struggles together. But an outsider would never have sensed any of that.

Finally, someone mentioned that the church was in deep debt. *Eureka!* That was it! The fact is, debt causes the kind of scene I was witnessing. It works against relationships. When payments are due and the money's not there, love vanishes, and pragmatism takes over.

After pastoring for twenty-three years, I decided I would never again be involved in any ministry or congregation that used debt to advance its growth. I'm convinced that with every dollar bought, the purity of love in a congregation is equally dissipated.

4. *Dishonesty.* Some time ago I received a rather stern letter from a couple I know well. In their note, they admonished me to take more care with the accuracy of the statistics that I share when I speak. They quickly added that I often make clear that my numbers are not complete. Still, they thought I should try harder to get them right.

They had me. The truth is, I'm not very good with numbers. Away from the crowd, I can remember whole sheets of them, analyze them, and talk intelligently about them. But if you tell me a number just as I'm going up to the platform, I'll surely get it backward, and I'll probably announce it higher than it actually is. (I know, I'm a true evangelist!) My mind trips over itself, and sometimes details get jumbled when I'm in front of a lot of people. The numbers I tended to get wrong were never critical to any decisions; those figures I would write down and read from notes. I guess I never really considered it a serious problem until I got this letter. Good relationships can only function when there is trust, and my sloppiness with numbers was breaking that trust.

I was reminded of the words of one of my favorite professors from Fuller Theological Seminary, J. E. Orr. "Doug, you're a good evangelist, and you're quick," he said, "but let me show you something." Then he pulled out a little book and opened it for me. In it, he had written the names of people he had ministered with and on what dates. He also had written the numbers of conversions that had occurred at each place.

"You need to present accurate statistics," he said. "And you need to ask where others get the statistics they give to you. A leader's relationship with people is always tied to trust." He held up his book. "This will help you always state the truth, to the number."

I thanked my friends for their letter. I told them that they were right. I had been sloppy, and I had injured relationships as a result. I promised them (and God) that from that point on, I would be on my knees making sure that all my numbers were absolutely correct.

Now I've just admitted to an area of inadvertent dishonesty. Do you have dishonesty in your life—purposeful or not? Have you shaded numbers, circumstances, or the statements of others for your own advantage? Have you been involved in backbiting or slander in order to make yourself appear better? Understand this: To continue will be to erode relationships. Dishonesty demolishes trust, and it works against health.

Churches cannot explode with healing in their communities if any of these four obstacles are working in their midst. On the contrary, churches that heal will nurture and protect environments where relationships are healthy and strong. When we major on relationships, true healing is bound to occur.

Wilt thou forgive that sin where I began, which was my sin, though it were done before? Wilt thou forgive that sin through which I ran, and do run still; though still I do deplore? When thou has done, thou hast not done, for I have more.

John Donne, "A Hymn to God the Father"

6

Becomers

As we move ahead I think it's important that we pause and ask ourselves, slowly, "Why should we heal at all?"

In finding the answer, the safest beginning point is to look at the ministry of Jesus. Obviously, healing was important to the Messiah. More than forty distinct physical and mental healings are noted in the four Gospel accounts. And if you count the duplicates that occurred throughout the New Testament, Jesus mentioned or discussed healing seventy-two times.

What were his motives for a healing ministry? Can we study his forty-plus healings and find a reason why churches today should seek to heal?

I won't take you through all forty, although it would make a fascinating study. I think our answers can be found by looking closely at just one: the healing of the ten lepers that was alluded to in the Introduction. I want to recount that story again and invite you to slowly walk through the scene. See if you can detect the motives behind Jesus' healing ministry:

> Now on his way to Jerusalem, Jesus traveled along the border between Samaria and Galilee. As he was going into a village, ten men who had leprosy met him. They stood at a distance and called out in a loud voice, "Jesus, Master, have pity on us!"
>
> When he saw them, he said, "Go, show yourselves to the priests." And as they went, they were cleansed.
>
> One of them, when he saw he was healed, came back, praising God in a loud voice. He threw himself at Jesus' feet and thanked him—and he was a Samaritan.
>
> Jesus asked, "Were not all ten cleansed? Where are the other nine? Was no one found to return and give praise to God except this foreigner?" Then he said to him, "Rise and go, your faith has made you well." (Luke 17:11–19)

WHY DID HE HEAL?

Did you see them? In this story I find five reasons that Jesus healed the lepers. You may see more. Certainly, he wasn't looking to increase his popularity; after all, nine of the ten lepers never even came back to say, "Thank you." He wasn't gunning for a great evangelism crusade; the healings took place after the lepers left. So why did he heal?

1. He was compassionate. Jesus took on the agony of the lepers' disease. These were people who lived along the border of Samaria and Judea. Exiled from society, their disease kept them at least half a football field away from others. They had to walk around in public crying, "Warning, warning! Unclean, unclean!" Imagine the shame riveted into one's soul by this process.

Jesus looked at them and healed them out of compassion.

2. He was hostile toward what makes people sick. Here and in several of Jesus' healings we see a brash, antagonistic, aggressive opposition to the cause of man's diseases. He turned these ten lepers into men who had skin like babies because he hated the thing that was destroying their lives.

3. *Healing was the right thing to do.* To heal is godly. Christ could not help but heal (except when God gave him clear instructions not to, as in the case of Lazarus). In Luke 4:18–19, he expressed his mission this way: "The Spirit of the Lord is on me...He has sent me to proclaim freedom for the prisoners and recovery of sight for the blind, to release the oppressed, to proclaim the year of the Lord's favor." Jesus healed because he could do nothing else.

4. *Healing brings glory to God.* Jesus wanted the understanding of what God was like to be enlarged in the eyes of those who were healed and those who observed the healing. His healing ministry pointed people to the Father.

5. *Healing helps to make us whole.* Being healed and being made whole are not necessarily the same thing. Healing can fix what's broken in our bodies or our minds. But God wants more for us. "Wholeness" describes a state in which everything about us is in right working order: our emotions, our self-esteem, our sense of morality, our thought patterns, our physical body, our spiritual faculties.

The one leper who returned to give praise was made whole. Thanksgiving, I'm convinced, is one of the pathways to wholeness, as well as the result. The other nine lepers were healed; their bodies were made free of disease. But the tenth man was made whole and complete, inwardly and outwardly.

It is God's ultimate aim for every one of us to be whole. He wants every portion of our being to be in peak operating condition, just the way he intended. That is the purpose of salvation, and he will continue the process until his coming.

The story of the ten lepers gives us clear guidelines for how to be made whole. Churches that heal need to understand and apply these guidelines. We need to encourage people, as Jesus did, to fully become the men and women God intended them to be.

Most of us live in a state of perpetual hesitation, and only by God's grace do we find the courage to step out and become all that God intended.

BECOMING WHOLE

Of course, salvation through faith in Christ is the critical first step for anyone who wants to be made whole. But the example of the tenth leper in Luke 17 shows us four steps to wholeness that we in the church can use to guide others.

1. Acknowledge your need. Clearly, all the lepers did this (vv. 12–13).
2. Be obedient to Christ and do what he tells you to do (v. 14).
3. Be thankful. Only the tenth leper expressed thanks (vv. 15–16), and he was the one who went on to wholeness. His praise was the ultimate expression of a healed and whole heart. Worship is always delightful when we've become totally operable.
4. Be ready to leave the old life behind. This man, the tenth leper, was willing to leave the other lepers and return to worship and follow Christ. In doing so, he received Christ's commendation and blessing.

Creating an Environment for "Becomers"

A church that heals understands that its mission is to see broken, hurting people become whole followers of Christ—new creations journeying into the full discovery of their identity in him. But too many people find that they can't "become" in the church they're in, and so they move from church to church, hoping to find an environment that won't be filled with obstacles to that process. This constant need to "move on" is a dangerous epidemic afflicting church life in America today.

Many move on because they feel stunted by a church environment that demands conformity or silences questions. Jesus respected every person he ever met; often the church doesn't. Prepackaged belief systems that deal with styles, opinions, and practices rather than the bedrock faith presented in the Bible become prisons for people, and healing stops.

Jim and Bobbie attend one of my new avant-garde churches in Seattle, and they love it. Nearly every week they tell me how refreshing it is to be part of a church where they can ask questions about why we do the things we do.

In tears, they recounted their previous experience in church leadership. In their old church they had noticed that many of the neighborhood folks who visited were visibly uncomfortable walking into the sanctuary in their jeans, T-shirts, and tennis shoes. So Jim and Bobbie decided to start dressing more casually, too, to make the visitors feel more comfortable.

On the first Sunday they showed up in jeans and Reeboks, however, the head elder quickly intercepted them.

"Leaders in this church don't dress that way," he said.

"But haven't you noticed how uncomfortable visitors are when they come in here? They can't afford to dress up," Jim said. "The neighborhood around the church has changed; it's not an affluent suburb anymore. The people are poor, and they need a church where they can feel at home."

"Now, Jim, that's what those new churches do," the elder chided. "These neighborhood folks are welcome, just as long as there aren't too many of them. We can't have our leaders affecting our growth by dressing for the wrong crowd."

The more stories Jim and Bobbie told me over time, the more I saw that their previous church allowed little liberty on any issue. Questions were discouraged. Healing just can't happen in such an environment.

One election year I was visited by a Democratic candidate for office. Jane had recently started attending our church, and she loved it. She assured me she was born again. She also said she was pro-choice when it came to abortion.

"Would you endorse me?" she asked.

"No," I said, "I never endorse candidates. But you are very welcome here, and when I introduce the other politicians from the church who are running for office, I will introduce you as well."

I then asked if I could go over some of her positions with her using the Bible as our guide. She agreed, and I proceeded carefully and respectfully, but truthfully. I explained that our official church position and my own adamant, personal stand was that abortion was the taking of a human life. I also assured her that I understood how women's-rights issues had become commingled with the abortion issue.

"I'm all for equality of the genders," I said, "but I believe abortion is one more way that women are exploited. I wish you could sit in on some of the hundreds of sessions our counselors have with young women who've exercised their 'choice' then found that it was destroying them from the inside out. This is too big an issue to leave to politicians, or even to judges," I concluded.

I wish I could say I converted her. In my younger days, I was highly political. But the longer I've been involved in evangelism, the more I've seen that a higher realm deserves the majority of my attention. Jane thanked me sincerely for our discussion and left.

On a Sunday not long before the elections, I asked all the people running for office to stand. We had four services that day, and we had politicians in each one. Some of the candidates were even running against each other! In the largest service, Jane stood up. I introduced her as the Democratic candidate.

I should have known. When I returned to my office Tuesday morning, one hundred letters from people ready to run me out of town were sitting on my desk.

"How do you want to handle this?" my assistant asked.

"Call a few of our leaders and fill them in. Ask them to pray for wisdom," I said. A few hours later, I knew what to do. We sent responses to each letter writer, thanking them for taking the time to contact us and asking them to show up at the next Sunday's service for a more complete response.

Sunday came fast that week. Word was out that I was going to apologize for being the endorser of a baby killer.

I strode to the platform. "In church last week," I began, "I introduced you to some politicians to pray for. One was a Democrat who began attending our church only a short time ago. If you treat her like some of you have treated me this last week, then I'm finding a new church!

"These are public services, and we are an outreach church. We are a church that accepts the sincere person into our worship setting. We are a church that listens—even to those we don't agree with. We are not afraid of wrong-headed ideas. We welcome the opportunity to be a biblical influence.

"I didn't endorse any candidate last week. We don't do that here. And I am strong in my opposition to abortion. What scares me is that so many people didn't take time to find these things out. They just made a judgment. We cannot heal the lost if we're going to exhibit the kind of uptight fear I've seen this week.

"I suggest that if you think we are too open, find a church that wants to spend all of its time deciding who's in and who's out. I've made a friend whom I'm committed to speak the truth to. I'm committed to helping her know what it means to fully experience Christ. If we take the step to follow him, none of us is going to stay the same; God's presence is going to transform us."

When I finished, I got a standing ovation! Some folks did choose to leave and find another church, but that's not always a bad thing. And by the next Tuesday, I had about fifteen letters on my desk complaining that I was too strong. Fear is a terrible thing!

Living in Love, Forgiveness, and Acceptance

I learned as a pastor that it's entirely possible to incarcerate people in their pasts. For example, if a fellow cheated on his wife twenty years ago, people still think of him as an adulterer. If a leader falls from grace, he's written off. Once a drug addict, always a drug addict. These are prisons that lock people into identities they've tried to leave behind.

We forget the fact that most of us need four, five, six, or more chances in order to finally grow into health.

A healer, I'm convinced, needs to have a bad memory.

In a healing church, people are not defined by the mistakes of their past. They're encouraged to grow beyond them. It's hard, deliberate work, but I see no reason entire congregations can't learn to give themselves to the task of helping one another "become."

In order to do this, love, forgiveness, and acceptance must be the watchwords. *Love* as demonstrated in a congregation is the magnanimous expression of many hearts living out the truth of 1 Corinthians 13. To love, the Bible says in essence, is to accept people the way they are and to celebrate whom God made them to be. Biblical love is unconditional; it sees that everyone is filled with the capacity to become someone wonderful—someone more like Jesus.

For its part, *forgiveness* is the central factor in emotional healing. To forgive means "to send away." Healers send people's sins away from them rather than repeatedly bringing them up. People today are broken, very broken. Their lives are filled with failure. Often, they can't go home without being reminded of the rotten person they used to be. Where can they go to receive forgiveness and healing? Nowhere but the church!

It boils down, then, to *acceptance*—the laying down of our right to place judgments and expectations upon people. Acceptance is not approval but a willingness to meet people where they are and encourage them to grow at their own pace rather than ours.

Acceptance is not tolerance either. For example, a Christian can never tolerate drug addiction in a fellow believer. But we can accept others and see them as people beyond their problems.

Chapter Six

Not long ago I received a letter from a man who had received Christ while I was pastor at Eastside Church.

> Before coming to Eastside, I was a mess. I was taking cocaine once in a while and drinking like a fish. My wife said she'd leave me if we didn't try going to church. She got Eastside's name out of the phone book, and one week we showed up.
>
> I wasn't ready for how down to earth you were! I was afraid to meet you because I was sure you'd be able to see right through me. The only time I got close to you was one Sunday when I wandered into the reception room where you had been praying with a group before the service. You didn't notice me; there were about ten other people in the room. You finished praying, stood up, and said, "Okay, do any of you want a good fistfight before I leave, in Jesus' name, because I can take ya!"
>
> One of the skinny pastors looked at me and laughed, "Don't mind him. He lives in his own world."
>
> It's funny, but at that moment I felt I could be that kind of Christian. Both my wife and I gave our lives to Christ. That was six years ago, and our lives have never been the same.
>
> My wife learned from the women's group that addictions may be difficult to conquer, but she also found out how to pray and how to draw boundaries so I could get healed. And together we saw that we were by no means the only couple with marriage problems, nor was I the only alcoholic under the age of thirty. Eventually I went through treatment. The lay pastors we'd met at Eastside visited me in the hospital, and people sent us cards telling us they were praying for us. I never went back to drugs or booze.

> We heard that you are starting some new churches. We don't feel we can come, but we want to encourage you. A few months ago we found a church that needed a volunteer youth leader. I'm filling that spot, and together my wife and I have already led many people to Christ.
>
> We just wanted you to know how much we appreciate you. We miss you and wish you God's blessing.

This was, of course, a very gratifying letter! I was especially glad to see how the whole church system had demonstrated love, forgiveness, and acceptance in the process of this couple's healing.

I've shared with you already that I inherited a wonderful gene that makes me manic-depressive. It stays under control because I do what the doctors say, discipline my thinking, and maintain my medication.

When I told my church about my diagnosis, I really didn't know what to expect. I thought they might write me off as a lunatic or leave the church for fear of…well, who knows what?

There's really no cause for fear. Today we know a great deal about chemical imbalance illnesses, and they're very treatable. We also know that King David, among other Bible characters, exhibited traits of manic-depression, and he was called a man after God's own heart! God is certainly not put off by such conditions.

The church surprised me. For the most part, they responded to my announcement with warmth, love, and strong acceptance. They encouraged me to continue to be open with them; when I was honest about my pain and struggles, they said, they felt like they could live with theirs too. And because of my openness, they knew that this was a church that wouldn't throw them out if they admitted to a struggle of their own.

Not that there weren't a few difficult times. After my announcement, some people on the leadership team had a tendency to put me "under the microscope," analyzing every detail of my behavior, rather than letting me "become." They tried to make sure I didn't express anything that smacked in the slightest of manic-depression. This close, fear-based scrutiny worked against healing. It was suffocating and harmful to me personally.

We had to keep dealing with it whenever it would start to rear its head. Everyone involved had to be reminded that the responsibility for staying healthy was mine, not theirs. The same thing often happens when alcoholics stop drinking; the people around them don't know how to let them "become"—how to let them be anything but an alcoholic.

This is one of the main principles we teach in our twelve-step program for the families of alcoholics: Let go, watch, and trust God. Churches that heal apply this principle in everything they do, creating an environment that is geared for "becoming." Whatever people are dealing with—whether it's a genetic illness like mine, alcoholism, a broken marriage, pride, sexual obsession, or anything else—they need a safe place where they can grow to be the people that God designed them to be.

Fortunately, most negative experiences, in the church and individual lives, have a silver lining. For example, my episode of being "microscoped" reminded me what it felt like to not be allowed to "become." Before that, I think I had forgotten the pain of not being accepted. I'm glad God allowed me to experience a mild amount of pain; it restored a great deal of compassion in my heart for others.

You know, we churchy folks often forget our own failings. We come to believe we've always been as strongly committed and devoted to the Lord as we are now. But almost certainly, when we get that smart and feel that sure of ourselves, we're in trouble. As Proverbs 16:18 says, "Pride goes before destruction, a haughty spirit before a fall." True healers and healing churches extend to others the same grace they've received.

BUILDING A "BECOMERS" COMMUNITY

Faith is nurtured when we see people change, grow, and become strong in the Lord. Whole congregations become humbly assured in their own salvation when people are allowed to "become." By seeking to build a community based on the principles of love, forgiveness, and acceptance, everyone wins.

How can you start to build a "becomers" community in your own church?

1. Express thanks to God regularly in services. Encourage people to give thanks for what they have and for what they are asking for. Thanksgiving keeps the human spirit humble. It's a key tool in the process of any healing.
2. Don't rehash the sins of members of your congregation. Allow their sins to be sealed in God's promise to forget.
3. Be open about your own weaknesses. Make sure that you and the entire leadership team model transparency and openness about your weaknesses as well as your strengths.
4. Think and teach frequently about the concept of becoming. None of us is an "arriver." We're all pilgrims and "becomers."

5. Allow the Holy Spirit to work. Make sure you never take the place of the Holy Spirit in anyone's life, but rather, with an attitude of joyous adventure, watch what God does through his mighty power in the people around you.

If we grab hold of these five keys, I have more than a hunch we'll see greater stability in churches in the future. Instead of seeing people move from church to church, remaining anonymous as they cover their pain, we will see people getting healed and becoming, in turn, the encouragers of others.

Watching one another "become," I'm convinced, is the most exciting part of being a church that heals.

Then Jesus came to them and said, "All authority in heaven and on earth has been given to me. Therefore go and make disciples of all nations, baptizing them in the name of the Father and of the Son and of the Holy Spirit, and teaching them to obey everything I have commanded you. And surely I am with you always, to the very end of the age."

Matthew 28:18–20

7

Is There Room in the Inn?

Something very profound happens in a congregation when we decide that making the message of Christ accessible and intelligible for newcomers takes precedence over our own needs. That priority, I believe, pleases God. And as we open our hearts to include the new, the lonely, the broken, we find that they are healed, and so are we.

My guess is that no more than 10 percent of the churches in the United States consider reaching new people their major focus. If you've ever had the opportunity to observe a highly evangelistic congregation, however, you've probably noticed that while the challenges are great, morale is higher there than in other places. People experience great joy when they participate in healing.

In my first church, we introduced between fifteen hundred and three thousand people to Christ annually. In the process, many longtime Christians joined us as well. Most believers, I think, are unaccustomed to seeing such a sustained concern for reaching the lost; but once they do, they become involved with great enthusiasm.

As one of our council members said, "I lived my whole Christian life without ever seeing anybody meet Christ—that is, until I saw it happening every week at Eastside Church. Now my spirit leaps every time a new person comes to the Lord, and my inner devotion to Christ has been accelerated."

Let's face it. Most of us are comfortable just having church with other church folks. It's a big leap to become a congregation geared toward sharing Christ with those who "don't get it." It's much easier to look at the troubled and broken people of the outside world and say, "Sorry. No room in the inn."

WHY SO MANY SEATS ARE EMPTY

Churches that heal are churches that make room. Today, some U.S. cities have fewer people per capita in church on Sundays than some Russian cities. In my own city of Seattle, the per capita church attendance is one-third less than the rest of the country! Surely there are seats in the sanctuaries, so why don't we fill them?

A Lack of Compassion

We need a wake-up call, something to shake us out of our apathy. Where's the compassion that led Christ to weep over the city of Jerusalem? Church people need to be reminded of the desperate spiritual state of the world around them. For example, in the United States alone:

- Two million people die every year. Only about 200,000 of those die knowing Jesus as their Savior.
- Loneliness is one of the major contributors to the high number of heart attacks.
- Each year 800,000 babies are born out of wedlock. That rate is just as high in the suburbs as the inner city.

Of course, I could cite pages of statistics like these. But the numbers are only the tip of the iceberg. For every pregnant teenager, there is a wounded family at home; for every drug addict, there is a confused and shattered father; for every husband addicted to pornography, there is a wife whose life is out of control.

A father once asked me in tears if I would consider visiting his son in a penitentiary. As he described how the young man had destroyed his life with drugs, the father broke down and wept. I agreed to make the extended drive. After all, the young man in prison represented far more than just a long trip for me; I knew his father, and I knew how much his father loved him.

I had a good conversation with the son. He didn't receive Christ, but he got choked up when I told him his father had broken down while talking about him. I found I really felt sorry for this kid who, at twenty-two, had so thoroughly messed up his life and hurt the ones who truly loved him.

Every derelict, thief, hooker, and addict has a mother, father, or someone who loves them. And even if no human being in the world loves them, they have a heavenly Father who does. Compassion can grow as we remind ourselves—daily, if necessary—that God is the Father of every man, woman, and child he has created. He loves them. He cares about them. He wants to invite them to be healed through our reaching out to them.

I encourage people who say they want to start leading others to Christ to get involved in a prison ministry or volunteer in an urban community center or children's hospital. Sometimes we cannot experience compassion for others because we become too insulated from real pain. And that lack of compassion is the major obstacle to becoming a healing church.

The "Us versus Them" Mentality

A real killer of compassion—and another obstacle to churches that want to heal—is an "us versus them" mentality that puts up false walls between believers and unbelievers. This mentality causes many Christians to view non-Christians with a sanctimonious attitude, as if to say, "I'm saved. You're not. Have a nice life."

Fortunately for us, this has never been God's attitude! Jesus Christ put on our flesh as a tent so he could show us what God was like. He discredited any "us versus them" mentality by identifying fully with us.

We, in turn, are called to be the body of Christ, a designation that identifies us with his incarnation. As the church, we are delegated to be his visible presence: Christians united to bring healing and wholeness, continuing his rescue mission to mankind. Our role is not to contend with the lost as if they were enemies but to identify with them as friends, bringing them to our friend and theirs, Jesus Christ.

I'm convinced the "us versus them" mentality is stifling outreach in most churches. It can be overcome, however, by a deliberate strategy that teaches Christians how to include their hurting neighbors in their spiritual experience.

As leaders, we must model our concern for the lost by including anecdotes in our preaching about our own encounters with broken people. One of the stories I often share with groups is about my own first time venturing out as a witness for Christ.

It was summer, and my hometown was celebrating one of its annual festivals in the public park—perfect ground, I figured, for my first attempt at witnessing. I boldly walked up to three or four students standing together, read one Bible verse, then told them how I'd met Christ.

When they seemed interested, I proceeded to tell them a few more testimonies I'd heard some of my friends share. I'd only been a Christian for three weeks, so my portfolio was limited! My advantage was that I hadn't been around long enough for anyone to tell me how hard witnessing was or to warn me that people wouldn't respond.

The four students, who were part of a high-school marching band, called together about eighty of their band members and said, "Hey, come listen to this guy." I jumped up on top of a cannon—some kind of town monument—and went through the story again, explaining who Jesus was and how they could know him. Then I asked, "How many of you want to receive Christ?" All but two or three did. So I asked the question again. I couldn't believe so many had responded!

The only problem was, I didn't know how to pray with them to receive Christ. My own conversion had not been particularly orthodox, so I wasn't sure how to proceed.

I did the only thing I could think to do: I told them to follow me up the hill to the Christian coffee house located about a block from the park. I marched in the door with sixty-five band members (we lost about fifteen stragglers along the way) and asked for the director. He led them all to receive Christ and the blessing of the Holy Spirit.

Afterward he whispered to me, "How'd you do this?"

"I don't know," I shrugged.

Whenever I share that story, people love it, even if they've heard it many times. It's the story of somebody who knew nothing doing something simple, and people responded.

I also like to tell about the lawyer who had been taking care of some legal matters for our congregation some years ago. One day when I arrived at his office, he ushered me in, closed the door, told his secretary to turn the meter off, and began to pour out his heart.

"I don't know what it is," he sobbed, "but I know that you have something, and I'd like to experience it." So I led him in a prayer to receive Jesus.

When we share stories like this, the congregation sees that the pastor is having encounters with lost people in the course of his everyday life. The same kind of thing could just as easily happen to them! It also helps them to see that every person they meet could, in fact, be someone who is open to hearing about the Lord.

A *Lack of Transparency*

A third obstacle to reaching and healing the lost is a lack of transparency on our part. People today are skeptical and cynical about just about everything, and especially about church leaders. We *must* live our lives in the open. If we're not transparent, people are going to see right through us anyway!

Our daughter has cerebral palsy. Deb and I have raised her joyously, as the people we've pastored could tell you. All along they knew what she faced and what we faced and how we've overcome all the hurdles together through Christ. Today she is a brilliant, active young woman with a dynamic faith of her own. Because we've been open about the struggles, many people have been encouraged and blessed.

Several years ago I also began sharing about my struggle with manic-depression. It has been a learning process for all of us as we've come to understand more and more about mood swings and the medications that control them.

That openness has paid off. Here's just one letter I've received over the years:

Pastor Doug,

Please don't stop being transparent. I didn't know what was wrong with me my whole life. I just seemed irritable, and no one wanted to be around me. Every once in a while, my life would get out of control. But when you began to share how you found out you were manic-depressive, as well as some of the things you learned that kept you whole, I began to realize I was suffering with the same thing.

I made an appointment with a doctor, and we talked through my problems. Sure enough, he said, "You've got a great pastor there, and you should go thank him. By sharing his life, he's offered you an opportunity to raise the quality of your own."

When leaders live transparently, the members of their churches learn to follow their lead. As a result, skeptics and cynics who come in the doors expecting hypocrisy or shallowness are soon disarmed. Hurting people, afraid that no one will understand their pain, are quickly put at ease. The environment is primed for salvation and healing to occur.

A Consumer Mentality

Probably the most difficult obstacle to reaching the lost is the stunning percentage of Christians who view church as a place to have their own needs met rather than a place where they can sacrifice themselves for Christ's cause. Over the last thirty years or so, we have created church "consumers" rather than radical participants. And in the process, we have cut off our ability to heal.

This "consumer mentality" is the cause of the tremendous turnover that's troubling many local churches today. In every city, there are multitudes of Christians who just keep moving from one church to another. They've developed a fine sense of when it's time to move on in order to avoid character development. Rather than face issues and deal with problems, they simply pick up and look for the next easy or exciting place to go. Meanwhile, churches become progressively less effective at healing as they spend their time and energy competing to hold on to these rovers.

In my city of Seattle, nearly every church has a turnover of between 20 and 30 percent every year. Any church that grows by 10 percent has actually replaced the third that left and has managed to increase beyond that. There could easily be 40 percent new people in that congregation—a seldom-seen feat in this day and age.

By failing to denounce consumer Christianity, we are encouraging believers to become self-serving—a deadly killer of compassion. We are also setting up pastors and church leaders to become proprietors of a "religious business" that must keep the "customer" happy at all times. That's impossible, of course. And unless this trend is somehow averted, I believe we are nearing a major implosion. Making disciples must be our goal, not satisfying consumers.

Right now I am starting four new church sites at once—yes, four brand-spanking-new congregations. And at forty-seven years old, this is a significant undertaking for me. But I love developing new innovations in church life and teaching new congregations to reach out to their communities.

In the process, I bet I've had at least seventy-five calls from people saying they're glad I am doing these churches. But they quickly add that in terms of their own involvement, they feel they are unable to be part of a new church plant where nothing is set up for them.

"As soon as things are more settled and the programs are in place, we'll be there," they say.

I don't take it personally. I love my friends, and they can do what they please. I will always think the highest of them. Besides, I really believe that we are called to churches; we don't choose them. This is a fact that few Christians understand. Why would God call highly qualified, committed, active believers to a completely new church that has a part-time pastor, a rented storefront room, and not much else? To help, of course!

Maybe these folks are not called. That's okay. But I do have a concern with the little phrase, "We need things set up for us." Why do we need things set up? Are "all the right programs" really what makes a church? I know they're not the stuff that makes a healing church.

One middle-aged businessman and his well-dressed wife met with me after coming to a number of the new church meetings. "Wherever we go to church, we really like to have the pastor come down and bless our business after church on Sunday then have a special meal at our home," the husband told me.

"Well," I said, "at this point I do four services a weekend, and I often fly out on Mondays to do conferences and other things. I can only do so much! But I bet one of our area home-group leaders would love to pray over your business and come to your home some Sunday. That way, you can meet someone who can really help you and be there for you on a consistent basis."

As I spoke, I noticed their expressions beginning to tighten up. It hit me that they had a specific idea in mind for what a pastor should be and do, and I wasn't fitting.

"Well, my wife and I feel you are supposed to be our pastor," he bore in, "and this is one of our real needs. We need to feel that our pastor understands and appreciates that our business is a gift from God."

I bristled. I always hate it whenever I sense that wealthy Christians are making demands based on their giving.

"If you are here at this church, you haven't joined me. You've joined the whole church," I said. "All of our leaders are your leaders. And besides, if I do what would be harmful to me and my family, given the realities of my limitations, I would be disobeying God."

I took a deep breath and continued. "If you are aligned with this church, I would hope you are here to serve and that you'd endeavor to do what's best for the church as a whole. Please understand, I cannot do what you ask. But let me suggest something else. We have an outreach going on from now through Wednesday. Why don't we sit down and have some coffee after the meeting Wednesday night and get to know one another better?"

The eyes of my new friends were sad.

"Well, we signed up for a class at another church on Wednesday nights," the man said with a tone that sounded whipped. "We won't be available on Wednesdays for several months." He had never been told no in church, I could tell.

"Great," I said. "Let's make a date for a couple of months from now. In the meantime, I hope you understand that our congregation is about outreach and healing. We really do expect that we will each follow Christ sacrificially, without regard for our own needs."

As you can imagine, this couple didn't hang around long. They were fine people, and they loved the Lord. But they were like so many American Christians—consumers seeking the best product rather than disciples following God's will.

Sacrificial Christianity

One of my best friends in the world is Dr. Lucky Klopp. Dr. Klopp has been a church consultant for a long time. In the very early years of my last pastorate, before I knew him, he stopped by my office. I asked one of our interns to meet with him. I was deep in study, and I didn't have time to drop everything for a visitor I knew nothing about.

When the intern told Dr. Klopp that I couldn't meet with him because I was preparing and praying for Sunday, he was thrilled. He had just completed some research showing that this was the single factor common in all healthy and growing churches: The pastor was not always available but was given to prayer and serious preparation.

Dr. Klopp was searching for a church to serve in, and he wanted one that he could sacrifice for. The fact is, no church can be a healing church without a good-sized core of people who are willing to be disciples rather than consumers.

Teaching Members to Count the Cost

I'm convinced church leaders need to teach more on the cost of discipleship. Church membership ought to be more difficult. Several years ago, baby boomers began coming to church in huge numbers. More recently, they've been leaving just as quickly. One of the reasons, I've been told by many, is that they found church too easy. There wasn't enough action; it didn't demand enough.

At one point, when our church had reached an aggregate attendance of about five thousand, we determined to overhaul the membership program. We spent time teaching about what it means to be a church member, then asked the people if they were willing to make a pretty demanding commitment. We started rebuilding our membership roster with the first four hundred people who agreed to take the step.

We came up with five basic, but not necessarily easy, requirements that all members were asked to keep. There were no classes. Each person was interviewed one-on-one by a trained leader. After making sure they were in fact born again and had been baptized, we asked them to agree to

1. read five chapters of the Bible a day
2. pray ten minutes every day for the church and its ministry
3. seek to include friends and others in outreach events and the sharing of the gospel
4. volunteer at least four hours a month in care of the church facilities
5. belong to a small group

We decided that a "membership" would be two years in length; after that, a person had to reapply. The reasoning for this grew out of a long conversation I had with Bill Hybels, pastor at Willow Creek Community Church near Chicago. Bill and I noted that baby boomers, in particular, tend not to retain long-term commitments and needed to "re-up" at certain intervals. (This was not a recommitment to Christ, of course, but to the mission of a specific local church.)

Nearly thirteen hundred people signed up for the membership interview within the first three months. It took awhile to get to everyone. In fact, we seemed to stay behind by about seven hundred interviews all the time. There's no harm in making Christians wait on some things though. It's like waiting to get into a great restaurant;

you're not really bothered because you know how good the food is going to be!

Teaching about commitment and about the need for believers to give of themselves sacrificially creates an environment that anticipates God's power. Of course, such teaching must be done in sensitive and creative ways, especially with the slow-to-commit baby boomers. But it is critical that people learn that our churches do not exist as spiritual storefronts for browsing Christians but as places of shared experience, discipline, healing, and outreach.

Helping Members Become Involved

I know it took us some time to get our people to see that we were serious about reaching and healing the lost. Over the years, we devised a number of ways to involve our members in outreach efforts. Some of the most successful ways included:

"Bringer and includer" events—We printed free tickets for a special event and announced an apologetic theme—always something that would be of interest to unchurched people struggling to understand why they should believe. We planned great music and a creative presentation of the topic that would answer some of people's most troubling questions.

We made sure our members understood that the evening would not be geared toward believers, but toward the lost. Our people responded well and invited their unsaved friends, relatives, and acquaintances. In the process, they learned how to lead others to Christ.

Special Sunday services dealing with apologetic themes—One of the best-selling tapes we have in our catalog is titled "How We Got the Bible, and Why We Know It's the Word of God." It's a theme that's aimed directly at someone who is struggling with the Bible as an authority base. We found that this and other apologetic topics were good to address from the pulpit from time to time. Not only were they good teachings for newcomers, they helped Christians know why they believe what they believe and gave them tools for witnessing to others.

Musical outreach—We attempted to do one or two musical outreach events every year. Christmas, we found, was the best time; after that, around Easter. People brought friends and coworkers, and it was not unusual to see one hundred people come to Christ in a single evening.

A HEALING DYNAMO

Churches that reach out to their communities in this way become healing dynamos. When believers share Christ with others, it not only changes the other person's life, it builds a dynamic faith in the Christian!

The key is sacrificial giving—putting our own interests aside in order to make room for new people. That sacrifice releases healing in others as well as in us. Giving is the only prescription for a hardened heart. Selfish Christians who begin sharing their church life with others are healed of the spiritual and sometimes even physical maladies that have built up in their lives.

Consumers, on the other hand, heal no one. Those Christians who are looking for the perfect church but don't want to work to develop it live with many spiritual cancers inside them. How Christ would like to break through and heal them by turning their eyes away from themselves and onto the lost and hurting!

Studies have shown that when people who are chronically depressed are encouraged to help someone who is far worse off, they get better quicker. There's just something about getting our focus away from ourselves and onto others that accelerates healing.

We do this one step at a time. In fact, I think compassion for others builds in the human heart in somewhat the reverse way that calluses develop on our fingers. I play guitar addictively, writing choruses and trying to impress myself. Over the years I've slowly and painstakingly developed some very deep calluses. I think these are parallel to some of the calluses that cover the hearts of consumer Christians. Hardness is compounded when concern for the lost wanes.

Not long ago, I decided to impress my wife and daughter with my toughness by lighting a match and holding the flame under my fingers. I could not feel any pain at all; in fact, I did some damage to a fingertip without knowing it. My fingers were so desensitized I couldn't even feel the fire anymore.

The only way we can heal a callused heart is by doing one compassionate, loving act at a time. Evangelism dissolves the calluses; our hearts are tenderized, and we are able to heal.

Our church decided to reach out to the most broken and hurting people in our community by starting a program we called "Lifeline." It began with a twelve-step program for the recovery of alcoholics and eventually grew into eighteen twelve-step programs geared to various life problems. It became a side door into the church; people who attended the Lifeline programs often met Christ then started coming to Sunday services. Just hosting this program seemed to tenderize the hearts of our members toward the lost. It also gave them an avenue to put their newly found concern into action.

To be honest, there *was* some "getting used to it" involved. One of the issues we had to address early on was smoking in the meeting rooms. Up to that point, the church facility had been mostly a "smoke-free" environment. But people who are weaning themselves from addictions often substitute caffeine or nicotine for their more harmful drug habits. Many of the Lifeline participants were smokers.

We talked with the twelve-step group, explaining that we understood their healing process. We also told them that small children used those same rooms on Sundays and that we didn't want the residual smell of cigarettes to be overwhelming. The group discussed it and came up with their own rule: They would only smoke outside on the porch.

It wasn't but a week later that I got two or three irate calls from Christians who'd come to the church building for one purpose or another and seen people smoking and throwing the butts all over the sidewalks.

"If they're going to be on church property, they shouldn't smoke at all!" they complained. Gently I explained that we had to sacrifice to reach out.

Obviously, becoming a church that heals doesn't solve all church problems. It creates some of its own. But these are the kinds of problems we want—problems that bring us to God, because only God, working his compassionate heart through us, can solve them.

Oh Lord, grant us grace to desire thee with a whole heart, so that so desiring, we may find thee, and so finding may love thee, and loving thee, may hate those sins which separate of us from thee; for the sake of Jesus Christ, Amen.

———— ■ ————

St. Anselm

8

Just People

My friend Jerry Cook tells a humorous story, which he recounts in his book *Love, Acceptance, and Forgiveness*. A person in his congregation asked for permission to organize a group for divorced people. Trying to sell the idea, the person noted that it would not only be good for the attendees but would also benefit the church, since everyone would then know who all the divorced people in the congregation were.

"Well, would you like to have a special section where all the divorced folks could sit?" Jerry asked.

"Maybe that wouldn't be a bad idea," the person replied.

Jerry pointed to a corner of the sanctuary. "Well, then, let's have that corner over there for divorced people. In the opposite corner, we'll put former liars. Over here, we'll have the wife-beaters section." Jerry went on with his humorous portrayal of how a church ought not to be.

"I see what you mean, Pastor," the person smiled. "Let's forget it."

I'm convinced an essential characteristic of a healing church is a strong resistance to the very human tendency to categorize people.

White people, black people; old people, young people; rich people, poor people—we can hardly stop ourselves from playing the category game. Yet one of the first, giant steps away from love is to view a person as a representative or a statistic—something other than the unique individual God created.

I'm so concerned about this that I've even come to question most age-group classifications for worship meetings, Sunday-school classes, small groups, and other church gatherings. It's tragic when a church makes generalizations about seniors or reacts to twenty-somethings with preconceived ideas.

People are people. They are not categories. They cannot be painted with broad brush strokes. They are unique, created with precise, God-given personalities, gifts, and dreams that only they can achieve. A congregation that recognizes the individuality of its people will heal many.

The enemy wants us to put people in boxes; then he can put a lid on the whole lot of them. God, on the other hand, wants each person to be free to live the life that he's planned. But do our churches allow this process?

FEELING THEIR PAIN

Several years ago someone handed me a tape by author and educator Tony Campolo. Dr. Campolo told a story about a university course he taught on ethics. In one particular class, he was presenting the ethics of Jesus when he paused and asked, "How do you think Jesus felt about the prostitute Mary Magdalene?"

No one responded. Finally a Jewish student in the back of the room raised his hand. "He never saw one," he blurted out.

Campolo thought for a moment, not certain that the young man had understood the question or the text.

"Can you describe what you mean?"

"Yes," the student answered. "Jesus never saw a prostitute. He only saw a person."

What a gift that story has been to me over the years!

To be effective as healers, we can't have set in our minds that we're talking to a "wife abuser," or a "drug addict," or a "divorcée." If we're going to help, we must have compassion. We must sit in the other person's chair and feel his pain. We must see people, not problems.

The difficulty is that no two people—and therefore, no two situations—are ever the same. And if we don't see standard problems, we can't give pat answers. It isn't often that we get to use the same words of wisdom more than once.

I've had a few mind-twisters come my way in more than twenty years of ministry. Once a young man who was more than halfway through a sex-change process was brought to me by a doctor involved in the case. The man had received Christ in our services and had a dramatic conversion. He and the doctor wanted to know what the Bible had to say about his situation.

I couldn't hide my stunned expression as they told me the story. But compassion rose up within me, and I found myself feeling a deep responsibility to care for this new convert.

I tried to think of anything in the past—any previous counseling session, any situation I'd helped solve—that could inform my thinking. No gems floated to the surface. I determined I would simply have to rely on what I thought Christ would do.

First, I told the young man that I accepted him and was proud to have him in our church. I explained that God had a plan for him and was involved now in his every decision. Then I suggested that we follow Paul's instructions in 1 Corinthians 7:20: "Each one should remain in the situation which he was in when God called him." We ended our session by discussing his medical plan and the lifestyle he would now lead as a new believer.

Admittedly, that was an unusual situation. But even when many people have the same basic problem, a healer must look at each sufferer as an individual.

If you ever have had cause to interact with someone who has "fetal alcohol syndrome," you know how complex and frightening the disorder can be to deal with. In this syndrome, a pregnant woman's abuse of alcohol or illegal drugs causes damage to the part of her unborn child's brain that provides motivation and processes right and wrong. As a result, these kids can grow up to be very difficult and unpredictable. They can be the sweetest guys in the world one day—and something quite different the next.

Given the prevalence of drug abuse on the streets of America, I wonder if many street kids and young adults aren't affected by this syndrome. In fact, when I meet teenagers or twenty-somethings who can't pay attention at school or work, who run away from responsibility or get involved in criminal behavior, who can't maintain a job or any other commitment, I'm not surprised if I find out they suffer from this malady.

I have sought out the best medical and psychiatric advice available to learn how to help people with this syndrome. As far as the world is concerned, however, there's no real treatment. And the church's customary "Gospel Gus" approach is of no value with these young people. So I've had to ask the Holy Spirit to give me specific wisdom to help them—one at a time.

Seeing Down to the Heart

I am an avid student of data collection. I believe it has a valuable place in the church. *Demographics*—the vital statistics of a particular population, including such things as average age, income, education, and so on—are a great tool for designing programs and understanding the length and breadth of a church's reach. And *psychographics*—the study of the attitudes and values of a particular group—can add additional insight into how a church can most effectively communicate the gospel to its community.

I study both demographics and psychographics very attentively in planting and leading churches. Yet I make sure that when I leave the planning room, I leave all the numbers behind. The danger of an overstudied approach is that it leads to seeing the forest but not the trees. (Remember the blind man in Mark 8:24, partially healed, who told Jesus, "I see people; they look like trees walking around.") Sterile data can in no way reflect the individual battles and scars that life has inflicted on those we seek to heal. Healing that comes from the heart cares little for stats or numbers and celebrates each individual healing.

Still, we can learn much from relevant data. Studies show that most people who are successfully assimilated into a church felt in the beginning that they were a lot like the majority of the people there, whether that "majority" was defined in terms of race, socioeconomic status, educational status, or even geography.

But I can't help asking myself from time to time: Wouldn't it be terrific if there were a church simply for *people*—not *this* kind of people or *that* kind of people, but just *people?* I suppose that's not likely; God has clearly created us with different languages and cultures, and it wouldn't be realistic not to recognize them. But it is possible, I believe, to see through our differences to our hearts, and those are all the same wherever we are found.

The ten lepers in Luke 17 were a mixed crowd of both Jews and Samaritans, two races that typically had little to do with one another. But these broken men were one in their pain, knit together by their flaky skin, gnarled appendages, and years of rejection by society. It is likely that one race could not be told from the other in any physical way.

In the end, all people cry the same. All people heal slowly in the same places.

Jesus' disciples were probably stunned when the Lord stopped and not only talked to the lepers but actually healed them. They saw lepers; Jesus saw individual hearts.

Like Jesus, healing churches see people, not statistics. They help people understand that their badge of membership is not their race, their intelligence, their income, or any other demographic factor. Rather, they belong because their pain has been recognized, acknowledged, and appreciated for its awful power in their lives and because Christ has overcome it through the cross.

We are all simply people that Jesus died for. Our unity, ultimately, is found in the fact that our pain has been healed by Christ.

WOULD JESUS SEE HOMOSEXUALS?

One of the great lies of our last two decades is that there is such a thing as a "gay lifestyle." Actually, the gay lifestyle represents habitual behaviors that break God's law.

It is, in fact, an addiction.

I've often wondered if people who end up with distorted sexual identities are looking for an identity in a group to escape the people they are. I don't know, but I think it's a possibility.

We had an extremely effective outreach to homosexuals in my previous congregation. It was not publicized, and the congregation as a whole did not know who was or was not a part of it. The only people who were really aware of the ministry were our pastoral team, who directed individuals to the group.

This outreach had a phenomenal success rate, with a very high percentage of men and women turning from their homosexual habits and finding joy in biblical sexual behavior and ethics. The anonymity helped, but I believe the true strength of the ministry was that the group leaders never saw "gay people." They saw persons in pain and individuals who needed help.

Homophobia is a real problem for the church. Whenever we cease to see the people behind the sinful activities, we lose our power to heal.

I have known many homosexuals over the years, from my younger years when I was involved in the music scene to the last two decades of ministry and community involvement in greater Seattle. I feel about gay people like I do about married couples caught in adultery. I see hurting individuals, and I recognize their pain.

I was called to a hospital to minister to one of the first AIDS patients in Seattle in the early eighties. Joe had been a Christian in a large fundamentalist church. He had even brought a large number of people to Christ in his heyday. But then the pastor, whom Joe had held in hero status, fell into promiscuity and shattered Joe's trust.

"I just couldn't find faith anymore," Joe said, "and church seemed so distant to me. I would reach out, but it was like faith kept moving just a little farther than I could reach. I started drinking, and it helped ease the emptiness for about half a year." He stopped and looked directly into my eyes. Most of my face was covered by a mask, and I was wearing something that looked like a spacesuit. They didn't know much about AIDS in those days.

"I know most people like to know how I became a queer. That's why I'm telling you all this," he said, pausing to see if I would pass the test.

"I don't really care about that," I said without flinching. "But I think it might help you to talk, and I would know how to pray more accurately too."

"Okay," he said, then continued. "When I first met some gay friends, I found that they didn't try to put on appearances. They just included me in their world without question. Later, I found that drug addicts were the same way.

"I really miss what I had in Christ, but I'm dying now, and I guess I have lost it for good. What do you think?"

He was crying now. Purplish sarcomas covered his face. He had little substance beyond his skeleton. I cried too. He was a child of the church, hurt by our own.

The hospital staff had told me to keep my gloves on, but I took mine off to place my hands upon his forehead to pray for him. He committed his life to Christ anew, and the joy that filled him was very apparent. He asked if I'd come back. I did, three times before he died.

It is amazing to me how many homosexuals come from fundamentalist religious backgrounds. It is also amazing how much abuse takes place in the homes of fundamentalist families compared to the rest of society. The explanation, I think, has to do with their emphasis on "right behavior," which sometimes becomes a precondition to acceptance and love.

On the other hand, there's something very disarming about a healing church's refusal to identify people by their sins. People caught in tragic habits can sense when they come into a congregation whether they are being identified by what they've done wrong or by the image that God has given them. Their barriers go down when they recognize an environment of unconditional love. And in such an environment, they can be healed.

The Young and the Elderly

Once I visited the one-room schoolhouse my nieces attended in the mountains of central Washington. It was exactly like *Little House on the Prairie*. The little first- and second-graders were being helped by the big high schoolers; everyone seemed respectful of one another, and the teacher was smiling—something I don't recall from my own school days!

There's a genius there, I think, that we miss in most educational environments. In that one-room schoolhouse, the older kids were models for the younger kids, and the younger kids helped train the older kids for adulthood. Clear bonds formed across generational lines. Everyone benefited.

One of my main concerns with our schools today is that they are too big. Another concern is that we do boneheaded things like putting all the junior-high kids together in one building. A whole campus full of awkward, pimply adolescents experimenting to find their identity—it's a gruesome sight. Whose bright idea was that anyway?

I think the church ought to be more like a multigenerational, one-room school. But to arrive at that conclusion, I've had to make a real adjustment in my thinking.

When I was pastor at Eastside, our aim was to specifically reach out to baby boomers (and their kids) who had pretty much written off church as something irrelevant to their lives. As we grew over the years, however, we found that we also reached an amazingly large number of seventy-plus people. These older folks loved the sermons, they loved our music, and they were completely supportive of what Eastside was doing.

From them I learned that a mission to reach baby boomers is not about age categories; it's about a culture. People from a variety of age groups feel very comfortable with this approach.

I'm convinced elderly people need to be around younger people. And younger people need to be around older Christians. A healing philosophy of ministry will gradually reach a broad span of age groups.

At one point I began to notice that many of the older people at Eastside seemed to feel excluded from the hands-on, "blood-and-guts" ministry of the church. Participation was geared toward the younger people, they felt, and they settled on being spectators.

To counter this, I prepared messages on how we could blend all of our unique abilities and age/experience mixes together for the good of all. I made it clear that I did not view older people as part of an age-group category but as unique persons in Christ. Every person is in a "becoming" process, I said, expressing the life of Christ as he has designed. It wasn't long after that series that I began to see a positive change.

I'll tell you a secret that probably helped make the difference: I really like older people. I find it very relaxing and inspiring to talk over coffee with someone forty years my senior, especially if the person is a "forever learner." My granddad was like that, and he was my hero. I think hanging around with him helped me see the power of old age.

Don and Karlene were an elderly couple in our church. They had had a rough time raising their own kids during the era of the sixties, but they had learned a lot, and everyone had survived intact. Now they had a special love for twenty-something folks. When Don retired as an engineer, he started a small company and began mentoring young men and women in successful business practices.

"I can't be their father, nor would that be healthy," Don told me. "But I can help them see some things that would normally take them quite a long while to learn. I am a teacher!"

Don brought dozens of his understudies to church. And many met Christ.

He developed what he called the "Wisdom Pool." It was a home group that met for brief runs, comprised of twenty-somethings and retired folks. It was always popular.

Not only do churches benefit from interaction between people of different chronological ages, they benefit when Christians who are spiritually older connect with new believers, and vice versa. Sadly, in the hundreds of congregations that I have visited, it is usually apparent within minutes that the older, more mature Christians gravitate together, while the newer Christians, somewhat bewildered, often connect with the more undisciplined types who are willing to associate with them. As a result, the mature Christians don't discover the spiritual vitality that comes from connecting their lives with the lives of new believers, and the new believers miss the benefit of the older Christians' knowledge and experience, developing instead a misconception of how the church works.

Again and again, I've encountered long-term Christians who've complained, "We are leading too many people to Jesus here. When you speak, you focus too much on them. You need to speak more to the mature Christian."

Now I don't doubt that the latter could have been true. But I've always believed a preacher could go through cycles, swings, and emphases throughout a year and over the years in order to minister to everyone in a congregation. It takes a wise leadership team to identify the times to cycle in or out of a particular emphasis. None of us always hit it dead-on. We will never make everyone happy.

My response to such criticism has always been the same: "You actually will mature much, much more if you invest yourself in sharing what you've learned with new people rather than worrying about learning more yourself. It doesn't matter if the new person is old or young. Identify with them, then help them grow. You'll be surprised how much *you* will grow in the process."

Some of the best small groups I've seen—and some of the best churches—have been generationally mixed, and racially or culturally mixed as well. They've had a core of mature believers in addition to an ever-growing number of new converts. People loved each other and enjoyed each other's distinctives. They learned from one another and cared about one another's spiritual growth.

Just maybe, if we understand what Paul was saying in Romans 12 and 1 Corinthians 12, that's what we're called to be after all: the gathering of the dissimilar, in love, for the cause of Christ. That's a recipe, I'm convinced, for a healing church.

My soul is restless until it
rests in you, oh God.

———— ■ ————

St. Augustine

9

The Healing Journey

We people of faith have a great founding father in Abraham. This man, known to Christians and Jews alike as the "father of faith," left his home in Ur of the Chaldeans at God's command without knowing where he was going. He had a vague notion that he was on his way to develop a great nation for God, but he really didn't know where or how that was going to come about. Essentially, he was told by God to enjoy the journey—by enjoying the *God* of his journey.

Healing communities are those that aren't worried about "arriving." They enjoy the journey by enjoying the God of the journey. They understand that reaching perfection isn't something we need to fuss over; Jesus Christ is perfect, and by identifying with him, we know his nature will eventually emerge from within us. We lose our ability to heal, however, the moment we fail to see ourselves as journeyers and determine to settle in as a group of perfectly behaved people with absolutely perfect answers to every question. Churches that think they've "arrived" can heal no one.

Chapter Nine

The God of the Journey

We are headed somewhere; as Christians, we know this. There is a beginning to our journey as human beings and believers in Christ, and there is an end: the culmination of all time, and completeness in becoming like him. This Christian view of time is clearly *linear* rather than *cyclical*.

Hinduism, among other belief systems, promotes the idea of cyclical time, which essentially gets us nowhere. We keep circling around life again and again. The Romans held fast to this view of time. For them, life occurred and recurred, and no one knew exactly how or why.

On his journey, Abraham took the linear view. He knew he was going somewhere, and though he was not able to see the end of time, he was able to see the one who owns all time, God Almighty. Being a journeyer in the tradition of Abraham means having our eyes on the God of the journey. We can rest in the knowledge that the God of the universe, our loving Father, is the one who determines where we're going and how fast we'll get there.

As a pastor, I've encountered a tremendous fear of people "falling away" from the Christian faith—of people not "making it." When someone sins or seems to take a slide, or if they step out of ministry for a time, many of us assume the worst. The "backslider" has failed, we think, or perhaps the whole church has failed. But pass/fail is not the grading curve in the kingdom of God.

And if the one who falls is a leader, look out! But we should not be surprised when leaders, even in very visible ministries, need to take extended breaks in order to experience healing in their own lives. Dealing day-to-day with other people's life issues will take a toll on any pastor—plus the fact that some of those issues may have a measure of contagiousness. Jesus knew this; that is why he often retreated into the country. Unfortunately, church people rarely see the need to invest in their leader's health, and the leader pays.

It all comes down to how we view our journey and how we view ourselves in the midst of it. This is such a difficult issue for so many of us. If we don't understand that our life in Christ is a journey and that journeys by their very nature have ups and downs, starts and stops, days of sunshine and days of rain, we'll lose hope, both for ourselves and for others.

How are we going to help our fellow journeyers get back on the path when they stray unless we recognize that a bump in the road doesn't mean the end of the road? Churches that heal know that Christianity is neither cyclical nor fatalistic; throughout our lives we may need to be rescued again and again, but God will continue to lead us on that linear road to perfection in him.

Churches, I believe, must adapt a broad view of what it means to be "in Christ." We should have a paradigm-rich existence that marvels at how many different ways God describes us and looks at us—how many wonderful facets of our identity he leads us into.

Take a look at just a few of the paradigms you'll find in the New Testament describing the individual believer or the Christian community as a whole.

- We are God's sheep (John 10:14–15).
- We are his spokespersons, his witnesses (Acts 1:8).
- We are God's children (Romans 8:16).
- We are stewards or servants of Christ (1 Corinthians 4:1).

- We are the body of Christ (1 Corinthians 12:27).
- We are God's letter (2 Corinthians 3:3).
- We are his containers, his vessels (2 Corinthians 4:7).
- We are the family of God (Ephesians 3:14–15).
- We are the bride of Christ (Ephesians 5:25).
- We are living stones in the temple of God (1 Peter 2:5).
- We are pilgrims and strangers in this world (1 Peter 2:11).

These are only a sample of possibly hundreds of descriptions of who we are in Christ! We need to slowly, carefully think through each one—to put on each "uniform" and walk in it, considering what it is like. If we do this and train our churches to do this, I believe not only will our journey be richer but we will discover new, exciting, creative channels for helping others along the way.

A Fallen Couple

Over the years I've found myself in a "rescue and recovery" ministry. I often get the opportunity to clean up after would-be healers have unfortunately (and for the most part, unintentionally) harmed people who were depending upon them for spiritual counsel and help.

Once I was called by the mother of an eighteen-year-old young man who had become sexually involved with his girlfriend in the church. The two teenagers were convinced they were in love; in fact, they hoped to get married. Sex had seemed the obvious next step. But from that point on, things got more complicated.

Let's call her Susan and him Joe. As they sat down with Joe's mother in my office, I could see that they were still inordinately connected with one another emotionally. They sat very close and immediately began holding hands.

Susan began to tell me the story: About a year before, she had confided to her best friend that she was sexually involved with Joe. (She paused and looked at him with her adoring, sixteen-year-old eyes.) Her friend told the youth pastor, and the youth pastor told her parents. They were pretty simple, straight-laced folks, somewhat naive about the pressures of modern adolescent sexuality, and they blew up. Joe's parents were told as well.

With the support of both sets of parents, the pastor singled out the two teenagers in front of the whole youth group at their next meeting and exposed their sexual sin. Joe was kicked out of the group. (After all, he was eighteen and headed toward college.) They were also admonished never to see each other again.

Angry at her parents and humiliated by the church, Susan ran away to a nearby city and stayed away from home for six months. She called Joe regularly, asking him to come meet her. He had enough sense to refuse to go, begging her instead to come back home.

Two months before our meeting, Susan returned to her hometown and began to live with Joe's parents. Her own parents would have nothing to do with her because she had fallen so severely and embarrassed the entire family.

"What do you expect from me?" I asked, looking kindly at these two young people who'd gotten so off course. "How can I help you? Are you sure you don't need to go talk to the pastor of your parents' church together?"

"Oh no. Not that!" Susan responded emphatically. "I can't go through that again."

"Do you think it was right for the two of you to sleep together?" I asked.

They both responded timidly, but seriously, "Yes, we think it was."

I looked at Susan. "Yes, I know it was," she said passionately. "We love each other."

Switching gears, I said, "Okay. Let's identify what you felt when you were in front of the youth group. Did you feel guilty?"

"Of course," they both answered.

"You probably felt more ashamed than guilty, don't you think?" I asked.

"Yes, that's exactly it," they answered.

"And that hurts, doesn't it? It makes you feel bitter."

"Yes," they said in unison.

"Did it make you feel hopeless when they said you couldn't come back to the youth group?"

"Yes."

I then got a bit more bold. "Do you think they intended to make you feel hopeless?" I asked. "Do you think the church leaders stayed up all night looking for ways they could humiliate and shame you, or do you think they were trying to be firm enough to convince you to turn from sin?"

They both acknowledged that the church probably intended the latter.

"What if they were wrong? Not about what the Bible clearly says is wrong, but let's say they failed to approach you with gentleness, as Galatians 6:1 tells us we should when we try to restore one another."

Their eyes followed me intently.

"I bet your parents also have some regrets about the way everything was handled, even though they participated in it."

"Yes, we know they do," Joe admitted.

"So, why don't you just forgive them, the way you would want to be forgiven?" I asked. "Maybe this can be a learning experience for them too. We in churches sometimes make mistakes, even as leaders. It would be terrible for you to live your whole life in reaction to somebody else's mistake, wouldn't it?"

In the end, we all prayed together. Joe's mother offered a prayer that went something like this: "Dear God, we come to you in the name of Jesus Christ, our Lord, who forgave us for all of our mistakes. We ask that you help us forgive one another as we've been forgiven. We pray you would restore humility to the hearts of Susan and Joe and that they would seek to serve you purely and in wisdom.

"Lord, we also ask that you be with them as they go back to all the people involved and try to explain how badly their shame felt and how negative its consequences were and yet how badly they needed loving admonition and confrontation! We trust you to work this out, Lord."

We'd all been holding hands. I sensed the presence of God as we parted ways.

It was about two years later when a young man and woman came up to me after a service, both wearing wedding rings, looking like a normal, young married couple.

"Hi, Pastor Doug," the woman said. "We're going to be attending church here."

"Great," I responded. "I'm glad you're going to be with us."

They looked at me and smiled. "You don't remember us, do you?" the man said.

"Well, I think I do. You look very familiar," I admitted. Then it hit me. "Oh, you're Joe and Susan!"

"That's right," Susan laughed. "You know, after meeting with you, we went back and talked to the pastor at our church, and—remember, we talked about this?"

"Yes, I remember."

"The pastor admitted they had made a mistake in the way they handled our situation," Susan continued. "He had felt terrible about it and had been worried for us. We prayed together, then he forgave us and we forgave him. It became a great learning experience for everyone about how grace works."

"Now we're happily married," Joe added. "I've got a good job in my dad's company. Thanks for helping us see how this Christian life really is a journey. Sometimes we all get off track and just need a little help to get back on the right road."

"No problem, Joe," I smiled, relieved and happy that they, like the prodigal son, had "come to themselves" and found their way again. I put my arms around the both of them and prayed that God would bless their new marriage.

When we have a paradigm of Christian life that recognizes we're on a journey, in training, a letter still being written, or a family learning to grow together, we are more apt to trust in God's ability to heal and transform difficult situations. I have found that paradigm work is necessary in virtually every church that wants to heal. We all need a shift in perspective.

When hurting people come into what I call an "arrival-committed" environment as opposed to one that sees life as a journey, they tend to have one of three reactions: they *hide*, avoiding the light and remaining superficial; they *judge*, which is always a consequence of hiding from one's own sins; or they *pretend*, becoming hypocrites and putting on masks so others won't see the truth.

A healing environment allows people to pursue Christ authentically. It understands that people never mature when they hide and certainly don't grow in grace when they judge others. If they pretend, they never get healed. We need to look at our own churches with an uncompromising eye and determine to replace "arrival-committed" environments with those that are healing-friendly.

RUNNING THE RACE

Have you ever seen a late-night talk show host come up with a "stupid test" or count off a list of dumb statements in which each one is dumber than the one before? I've identified several stupid statements that many of us make in church—all of which stymie the forward progress of others and virtually guarantee that our churches won't heal.

- "If you just had more faith, you'd be healed." (Faith is definitely part of the equation in any healing, but it isn't 100 percent of it.)
- "If we just had more commitment around here, we wouldn't have so much sin." (Trust me, in today's addictive culture, even our commitments can be excessive and pathological. Healthy commitment is informed by the Bible, motivated by the Holy Spirit, and celebrated by the church. It comes from the inside out—not by demands from the outside in.)
- "The problem is, people in this church just aren't maturing." (The problem is, we all grow at different paces. Many breakdowns are caused by Christians being pushed to mature too quickly.)

- "We don't believe in psychology or psychiatry. We read only the Bible." (That's like saying we don't believe in computer science or physics. Now, I agree that we should not believe in *bad* physics and *bad* psychology. But there is psychology that is sound and biblically based. After all, God and his Word are the foundation of all true science. Saying the Bible is the only source we can read when we want to understand how our brain chemistry works is like saying the Bible is the source we should turn to when our computer breaks down.)
- "Good parents raise good kids." (No, no, no! What constitutes a "good kid" is a great question to visit, first of all. But I have known some really great parents who raised three or four remarkably spiritual children and then one knothead. If this statement were true, then we'd have to admit that God is an awful Father of the human race.)

Churches that heal don't make such statements. They hold humbly to the fact that we all are on a journey toward fullness in Christ; we all need restoring from time to time.

They also understand that we don't all start out at the same place. Some people test out of Christianity 101 and go straight to the advanced course. And one person's hard-fought snail's pace may bring just as much joy to God's heart as another person's more easily reached turbo speed. As the Bible says in 1 Samuel 16:7: "Man looks at the outward appearance, but the LORD looks at the heart."

Recently I found myself frustrated with a young man I was counseling who was dealing with sexual addiction. I was tempted to be very harsh with him. Then I discovered that he'd been homosexually abused for a number of years when growing up, and I had to change my tune. Of course, we now know through plenty of research that an abuser has often been abused himself. A large percentage of sexual addicts were sexually abused as children. This is often the case with prostitutes or women dealing with promiscuity.

Too often, we in the church look at someone who has a spiritual or emotional "broken leg" and tell them, "Run!" When they stand still, we wonder what's wrong with them.

We need to drop our unrealistic expectations and allow Christ to do his transforming work in the lives of others. A compassionate, healing community understands that "success" can only be measured by God. By his standards, the two small steps forward taken by a person dramatically debilitated by life may be a greater "success" than the circles some of us more "healthy" types might run around them.

I'm reminded of another biblical paradigm. Hebrews 12:1 says we are all runners in the race of life. And just as in any race, there are those who stand on the sidelines and cheer us on. As individuals, we run the race; as a church, we cheer each other on, encouraging one another to keep going to the finish line. If one of us stumbles, the cheering doesn't stop; instead, we call out even louder, "Come on, get up! You can do it! You're almost there!"

There's a sports saying you've probably heard: "It ain't over till the fat lady sings." For Christians, it's never over until life itself ends or Christ returns—that is, it's not over until *God* says it is. Churches that heal enjoy the journey and keep their eyes on the one who is waiting and cheering at the finish line.

The only way to keep your health is to eat what you don't want, drink what you don't like, and do what you'd rather not.

———— ■ ————

Mark Twain

10

Guilt-Free Zones

There's a community north of Seattle that is famous around our part of the world for declaring itself a "nuclear-free zone." The entrance to the town sports a monstrous sign declaring everyone's freedom from nukes within city limits. You may not bring nuclear weapons into the city of Bothell, Washington—and that's that.

The idea caught my imagination once, and I came up with a variation for churches. I think in the front driveway of every church there ought to be a large billboard that says, "Welcome to a Guilt-Free Zone."

You know, God wants Christians to be free from guilt. He hates guilt. Guilt is the child of the Fall, not a design of God's making.

Some confuse guilt with conviction and repentance, but they are not the same at all. "Feeling bad"—the predominant meaning of guilt, as well as the legal meaning of the word—never brings healing or freedom. It doesn't change our minds, and it rarely changes our actions (although we may adjust a little in order to ease the pain). On the other hand, when the Holy Spirit convinces us of our misdeeds (conviction) and calls us to turn from them through a change of mind (repentance), we may not feel anything; but we see the truth and respond by making a powerful course correction.

Unfortunately, many constricting forms of fundamentalism have learned to use the "guilt feeling" to shape the lives of their followers. But true repentance is a change based on solid information from the Bible. And it's the conviction of the Holy Spirit—not the pastor's skill at making us feel guilty—that empowers us to make a change and turn from our sinful ways.

How does guilt seep into my heart and your heart, especially after we've received Christ? I'm convinced that in a morbid way we are addicted to guilt. We've used guilt for so long as a personal motivator that we don't know how to live without it—that is, until we have been completely healed.

There are plenty of testimonials on daily talk shows decrying the terrible effects of guilt inflicted by parents or other authorities. Sufferers of virtually any malady, from cocaine addicts to mass murderers, are likely to blame their behavior on a guilt-imposing parent.

It's true that bad parenting can contribute to destructively low self-esteem. But aren't most of us growing weary of society's "victim mentality" that leads people to deny responsibility for their own behavior? Maturity is directly linked to owning responsibility. Sadly, we are a culture of broken children who've grown accustomed to guilt.

GUILT IN A CADILLAC CONVERTIBLE

One of the most interesting counseling sessions I had in the early days of Eastside Church was with a pastor's son. My own kids were not old enough at the time to realize the unique pressure they were under as children of a pastor. Thanks to their mother, they turned out great, and I praise God for that. But Deb had to have “the talk” with more than one Sunday-school teacher or youth leader over the years, admonishing them not to expect our children to be more than “just kids.”

Unfortunately, I’ve met far too many wounded pastors’ children. This fellow in my counseling session had watched his dad be treated thanklessly by their small-town congregation while he, his brothers, and his sisters got treated as the local buffoons. Every Saturday, he told me, his father forced the family to dress up (girls in dresses, boys in shirts and ties) and drive up and down Main Street, shouting a gospel of guilt and judgment through bullhorns.

“My word, how did you know what to say?” I asked.

“We were given scripts by our father that we repeated over and over.”

“Did anyone in the town fall on their knees in repentance or anything?”

“No, never,” he assured me.

I shook my head in amazement.

“Then, once we got tired of that,” he continued, “Dad would make us go to the movie theater and stand outside with the same bullhorns and scripts.”

“Lovely,” I said. “And then what happened?”

“Well, I was in junior high,” he said, “and Mondays at school were always really bad because all the kids had seen me with my bullhorn over the weekend. They called me ‘Daddy’s little preacher boy’ and a lot of worse things. That’s when I started to fight. I would just beat the tar out of those guys when they’d tease me.”

“Well, didn’t that undo all the preaching through the bullhorn?” I asked foolishly.

He peered at me over the top of his glasses, and from there our conversation got more intense. He told me that he joined the marines and began boxing in competition. He also became a sex addict. The stories he told me of his addictive life were horrific.

"Think back now," I said. "What do you think could have possibly driven you to such a lifestyle?"

"Just goes back to God and my dad, I guess," he shrugged. "Maybe I got involved in those things just to let some of the anger out. But I have never been free from guilt for not believing and following Christ. It's almost like I do what makes me feel more guilt because that's what I deserve."

Within this young man's story, I recognized an important truth: Guilt repels healing. And not only that, it actually forces us into a deeper pit, as the first seven chapters of Romans make clear. My friend had moved from guilt to shame: the sense that it wasn't just what he did that was bad; he was bad. And every church he'd ever reached out to for help had used more guilt as a tool to try to make him "better." All they accomplished, however, was to reinforce the shame he felt.

What he needed, I realized, was a church that understood that guilt is always present with sin. More guilt is not necessary! He needed to be convicted of the awfulness of his behavior by the Holy Spirit. He needed a reason to change his mind and repent. He needed hope that change was even possible.

And he needed to know that he had people who would stand by him and be his advocates in the process. Repentance, for this young man, would mean more than just coming forward for prayer during an altar call. It would mean getting some clinical help with his addictive behavior and making restitution where he had done damage. Any fool can feel guilty; only a repentant person does the hard stuff.

When I told him he needed to begin getting rid of the guilt in his life by returning to Christ and receiving his loving forgiveness, he balked.

"You don't understand," he said. "Our father made us feel guilty about even glancing at a TV in a friend's home. He made us feel guilty about having plenty to eat when there were so many poor people going without. I could hardly eat a meal! The guilt trip never stopped. It nearly killed our mother.

"I hate my father for all the guilt he made me feel inside. And now, added to that, is all the guilt I feel for the things I've done," he said, bristling. "I can't stand any church where they throw more guilt on the pile."

"Believe me, I don't want to add guilt; I want to remove it," I said. "I want to see it disappear through the forgiveness of Christ.

"Do you think you could be confusing your feelings of guilt and shame with conviction and a biblical conscience? They can feel very similar," I added. "Initially, the convicting work of the Holy Spirit can sting. But the Bible teaches us that true conviction about wrongdoing leads us to repentance, and that brings freedom.

"Shame and guilt say, 'You are wrong; therefore, you are bad.' The Holy Spirit says, 'You are in trouble, and I am your way out.'"

He looked hopeful. And after a number of prayer sessions together, he was able to begin to let go of the guilt that was drowning him and feel the freedom that comes from knowing the mercy and forgiveness of Christ.

Spotting Guilt

Years ago I received a fax from a woman expressing enthusiasm for my "irreligious nature." She said she'd been discouraged and wounded by churches she had attended in the past and had reached the point where she hated even the thought of going to church.

But she happened to stumble into our place with a friend one Sunday evening and found that she had entered a "guilt-free zone."

One of her statements rings in my ears even now. She wrote, "I wish everyone in your church and on your staff could be as willing as you are to let the Holy Spirit speak to me." She then went on to explain what she meant.

In that service I'd arranged for a nice couple to come to the platform, share a little of their testimony, and then pray before the offering. "That couple sounded quite religious," the woman wrote. (I hadn't noticed because I loved the people.) "It frightened me because they even made me feel a little guilty that I hadn't given in the offering."

Bells and whistles went off in my head! I realized that while I was careful to refrain from motivation-by-guilt, I had forgotten the importance of training others in guilt-free ministry. This is the value of having interaction with the newest people in your church: They see and hear things that we never would. We get used to each other's quirks, foibles, and sins.

I shot back a fax in response. I thanked her for the note and assured her that I detested using guilt as a motivation to do anything. A healthy church is a guilt-free church. We are free. As Jesus tells us in John 8:32, when we become his disciples, we will know the truth, and the truth will set us free.

Guilt is a cage that imprisons us, keeping us from being completely free and healed. When guilt is gone, we're like a bird being let out of the cage to fly. I know that's how I felt years ago when I was first freed of guilt through my newfound faith in Jesus Christ.

Unfortunately, we leaders know that we can get more done, raise more money, and move people more quickly by using guilt as a motivator than by leading in love and freedom. Health is slow. But guilt-free healing is God's way. It takes stamina to operate without using guilt—sometimes more than we have. But churches that heal must shun guilt and take the slow path.

I got a portfolio from a Christian college recently. They wanted me to know that they would go broke unless I joined a group of people to raise a million dollars. Now I'd never heard of this college, never gone there, nor had I known anyone who had gone there. No doubt it was a fine place. But they went for the "guilt jugular" with a front-page, full-color photo of some pretty rough-looking kids and the headline: "Do we really need to develop any more of these?" Across the bottom it read: "Give money to our college, and we won't!"

"Good grief," I said, tossing the folder in the trash.

I really believe we are about to see upheaval in churches and ministries that persist in teaching and leading by guilt. Churches today are at toxic levels of guilt. You can feel it in the air. Baby-boomer Christians in particular won't tolerate it.

Some time ago, as I was preparing the first in a series of sermons on the Ten Commandments, I stopped and asked myself, *Why were these commandments given anyway?* Even the apostle Paul, perhaps one of the most disciplined men that ever lived, said he could only fulfill nine of them: he couldn't keep the commandment against coveting. The fact is, no member of the human race can master all of the Ten Commandments! But that doesn't mean they should be ignored. Rather, they are God-given guides against which we can measure our lives and discover our need to be healed of guilt through grace.

In postmodern America, we've lost sight of how to live life according to a clear set of biblical principles and ethics that we are committed to even though we may fall short at times. Rather, the ethics of our times are the ethics of emotion. We try to become more and more spiritual, not by prayer or the shaping of our conscience by the Bible, but by emotional effort.

We don't heal people because we are not building ethical patterns into their lives; instead, we're encouraging emotionally driven decision making. Again and again, I hear young and old Christians say, "Well, I'm going to have to think about that and see if it feels like something the Lord wants me to do." Feeling supersedes truth in most bad decisions.

Now, I have no problem if the decision is whether to put pepper on your eggs. But many Christians make important decisions based on emotions when they have at hand the clear-cut truth of the Bible. This truth commands people not to live together when they're not married, for example—no matter how "right" it feels.

God gives us the patterns and principles, with lots of grace to go around. It doesn't matter how we feel about it. There is no such thing as morality-by-emotion.

Churches that heal must teach people to live according to the biblical training of their consciences, teaching right and wrong based on principle, not emotion. Guilt seeps in when emotions have sway. We feel the gauge on our inner "guilt meter" creep up until it gets us, at some point, to act. And preachers and other church leaders, trying to make people grow in the Lord, are often guilty of winding it up.

In certain situations, it's very tempting to pull out the trusty "guilt gun"—for example, when a church is in financial trouble. On several occasions when my own church struggled with a shortfall, there was always a well-meaning person who would grab me just as I was about to walk up to the platform. "You know, in my old church the pastor got everyone to give by making them feel really guilty," they'd wink.

I'd never say anything at those moments. I have a tough enough time conversing intelligently with anyone just before a service anyway. So I'd hold my peace. Then I'd go out and preach about grace. The Holy Spirit teaches us to give like Jesus taught us to give: out of love and obedience, not guilt.

But believe me, I'm not immune to the guilt trap. I had a couple visit me after a service not too many months ago. I'd preached a rousing sermon. I think I had gone into the pulpit mad about something—oh yes, that was the morning I'd pulled out of the driveway and backed into my daughter-in-law's car. I was definitely out of sorts, but it seemed to give real fire to my preaching.

"Pastor, I feel like I really grew in the Lord this morning," the husband told me. "I haven't felt that bad in a long time." His wife smiled and shook her head vigorously.

I was stopped in my tracks. This was bad—very bad. I thought back and realized that my fire-breathing sermon had been filled with some pretty mean "shoulds" and "oughts."

I had nailed people right and left, getting their guilt meter all wound up. I had tried to make them feel bad so that they'd do what I thought they should do. I had preached a guilt-driven Christianity.

The unfortunate part was that an awful lot of people really liked it.

I went upstairs to my office and fell down on my knees. I asked God to forgive me and help me be centered again on his grace.

Chapter Ten

Freeing People from Guilt

Churches that heal free people from unhealthy guilt. How can you begin to do this in your own congregation? Here are seven important steps:

1. *Avoid religiosity.* I've noticed—far too often—a pukey kind of formality that gets into some churches. It's not just a matter of service order or liturgy; rather, it's a mind-set that says, "This is the way the Holy Spirit works in our church." People are rejected or accepted on the basis of whether they conform to the pattern.

In my early years as a Christian, I struggled with church—that is, until the publishers came out with the Living Bible and then the New International Version. I never could understand the King James Version. I think that's because I've always been so pragmatic and down to earth. The "thees" and "thous" and "begats" just didn't work for me. And if something doesn't work, I don't get it.

I can remember being admonished for not reading the Bible from the King James. I was a young Christian, and the criticism really hurt. I didn't know then that I was in the clutches of a religious person.

Religion says, "I'll make myself good enough for God." True spirituality says, "Only through Christ can I make any claim to godliness." Religion says, "I can tell how well I'm doing spiritually by comparing myself to others." True spirituality says, "There can be no comparisons except our comparison to Christ."

2. *Teach the Word, and let the Word stand on its own.* I'm concerned that in many of our traditions, we're moving people to action by using the Word like a hammer. If we're not careful, our altar calls and other special appeals can become very emotional and guilt-inducing. Some border on crowd manipulation. A person needs to be able to relate to

Christ as an individual, not just as part of a mass appeal. We must remember what Paul said in 1 Corinthians 1:18: The message of the cross is powerful in itself. We don't have to embellish it or twist any guilt meters to get a response.

3. *Teach the law of love.* James 2:8 tells us to live out the "royal law" of love. Sharing, blessing, encouraging, and living out the loving spirit of Christ with one another leads to the fulfilling of the law. Correction, done in gentleness and the right spirit, may be included, but guilt is never part of the package.

Churches that heal teach people how to love. Love produces proper behavior in a way that guilt and manipulation never can.

4. *Let the Holy Spirit lead.* Getting out of the way and allowing the Holy Spirit to work in people's lives can involve both danger and joy. Danger, because being led by the Holy Spirit takes some practice and because many people, influenced by the goofy mismodels that abound in the church today, have the wrong idea of what it means to be influenced by the Spirit. A bit of confusion usually precedes arrival at a more biblically based approach.

The joy of letting the Holy Spirit work in and through the people of the church is that more things happen than you or I could ever take credit for. Morale rises when more than sermons are recognized as the Spirit's activity. People experience tremendous fulfillment when they sacrifice for the good of others and see the Holy Spirit minister through them.

5. *Allow people to grow at their own pace.* In his parable in Matthew 13:24–30, Jesus said that we shouldn't, in this life, try to separate wheat and weeds growing in the same field. Sometimes the weeds look so much like wheat stalks that you can end up pulling up the good stuff if you go after the weeds.

We shouldn't be so sure about our ability to discern the difference! (That's also why the Bible tells us in Matthew 18:16 to have "two or three witnesses" when we intend to bring a charge against someone. Can we be so sure we're not reading the situation incorrectly?)

We live in an age where we cannot always discern true spirituality when we see it. We should be humble and realize that grace moves everyone at different paces. What looks like a patch of weeds to us may mature into a beautifully white field in its own time.

I counseled a man once who had been sexually abused as a child in his own home. As is often the case when there's abuse, the lid blew off as he neared midlife. He became involved in a series of promiscuous relationships that nearly destroyed his family.

Someone found out about it and approached me. "How could he be so far from God?" the person asked. Not being able to tell the whole story, I think I understood at that moment how God must feel. "Maybe if you knew all he has gone through," I said, "you would feel differently."

6. *Keep the right records*. First Corinthians 13:5 says love "keeps no record of wrongs." The positive corollary would also be true: Love keeps long records of good things done.

Sometimes, as a pastor, I get fed up with the church. I feel like I'm trying to lead a bunch of nipping, clawing cats on the verge of a big brawl in the alley. But just when I decide I'm going to blast them and tell them everything they've done wrong, I catch myself.

Instead, from time to time, I read them a list of the things we've done right: We've ministered to needy people despite our own tight budgets. We've led many people to Christ. Marriages have been healed. Many have found freedom from addictions.

Churches that heal focus on things that are being done right. They don't badger people about their shortcomings.

7. *Neutralize guilt and shame with acceptance*. As we've noted, guilt says, "I know I've done something wrong in my past; therefore, I feel bad." Often guilt is free-floating in people's lives. It's as if the tether holding it to a specific incident has been cut loose, and it just bumps around in our minds, whispering "guilty, guilty" for some reason we can no longer remember.

I've been in innocent conversations when a story someone was telling caused me to blush and feel uncomfortable. Apparently there was some guilt related to that topic floating around in my mind.

Shame is guilt's much uglier cousin. It says, "I *do* bad things because I *am* a bad person." In every addictive pattern, you'll find a great deal of shame. The addictive behavior alleviates the pain of the shame but then reinforces it. It's a vicious cycle.

Churches that minister to alcoholics, drug abusers, or other addicts especially need to know how to neutralize shame and guilt. And the sure antidote is something we've talked about before: an atmosphere of love, forgiveness, and acceptance. In such an environment, we still contend for change. But we let people—particularly our children—know that they cannot lose our love through bad behavior.

People dealing with addiction may still relapse after receiving Christ. Though their behavior is not approved, they *must* be accepted when they return to the church. This acceptance gives them *hope*—the power to believe that they can overcome.

Those of us who love people get exasperated with them sometimes. But using guilt and shame to control their behavior is not Christlike. It's bogus. It never works for long.

Sometimes the people we help can only respond in part. That doesn't mean that our efforts are wasted. The hand outstretched to heal is never forgotten.

They come back to see you. I remember one man, a top player in the NBA, who had been caught in the grip of addiction. I had counseled him the best I could, but when he left my office I was convinced I hadn't been much help. I was wrong. Some time later he sought me out to say, "Thanks for believing in me. Thanks for caring. I've been sober for several years now."

Churches that heal do not resort to guilt. Rather, they lead people to Christ, where the ultimate in love, forgiveness, and acceptance is found. They model his life and trust him to do the work that's necessary in the lives of others. Churches that heal become true "guilt-free zones."

Whatever you say,
say it with conviction.

Mark Twain

11

Nurturing Optimism

If there's any area in which we are particularly sloppy as Christians, it's in our verbal and mental disciplines. Let's see what a healing church's thought life should look like, according to a little letter Paul wrote to some believers in a city filled with unsympathetic and menacing Roman soldiers: "Finally, brothers, whatever is true, whatever is noble, whatever is right, whatever is pure, whatever is lovely, whatever is admirable—if anything is excellent or praiseworthy—think about such things. Whatever you have learned or received or heard from me, or seen in me—put it into practice. And the God of peace will be with you" (Philippians 4:8–9).

In the verses preceding this section, Paul encouraged the Philippian Christians to be joyful despite their circumstances. "Rejoice in the Lord always," he wrote in Philippians 4:4. "I will say it again: Rejoice!" Being a community that rejoices, no matter what, is a critical characteristic of a healing church. But how do we get to be that way? You and I both know it doesn't come naturally!

Chapter Eleven

Six Habits of Christian Thought

Following his commandment to rejoice, Paul gives the key: six habits of Christian thought, six simple little practices that renew our minds and ultimately enable us to rejoice, to heal, and to be healed.

1. Think about those things—"whatever" (in the Greek, hozasa)*—that are in harmony with a Christian mind-set.* Essentially, Paul says that whenever you come across a thought that has the right "nutrients" for a healthy soul, latch on to it. Let go of anything that doesn't help you think and become more like Christ. Christians must be discriminating thought consumers. Careless words and ideas fly fast and furiously in our time—in the church as well as in the world. Be wise.

2. Think with discernment—"true" (in the Greek, alethe). Truth, as described here, analyzes authenticity. Not all things are authentic. There are a lot of things that are true to fact but are not *true*. We must believe everything that Jesus says, and we must think about anything that represents the truth as seen in him. Then we must concentrate on what we have established as known fact and indelibly imprint it on our brains.

Churches that heal don't spend a lot of time on nebulous ideas, evaluating and reevaluating those things that have no scriptural basis. They don't get involved in speculation or "foolish controversies and genealogies" (Titus 3:9). Their minds are trained to think carefully, objectively, and alertly about this world.

3. Think honorable thoughts—"noble" (in the Greek, sebo). Honorable, or noble, thinking is the kind of thinking that makes you worship. It causes you to revere with awe what God has done in you and around you. Noble Christian thinking makes itself busy about those things that cause us to live in the realm of praise and thanksgiving.

The negative corollary is to live as habitual complainers or critics of God's work.

On one occasion, as I prepared to teach on this subject, I stopped to examine my own thinking before heading off to the event. I realized my mind had become stuck on thinking about a person I'd had a run-in with who seemed quite difficult and strange.

As I flipped open my Bible, my eyes fell on Ephesians 2:10: "For we are God's workmanship." It was almost as if I heard Paul say, "You know, Doug, we're all created as a wonderful poem of God. We're all his artwork." I was inspired at that moment to recognize that although the man I'd argued with seemed eccentric to me, he was God's work of art, and I needed to appreciate him as such.

All of us have been on the other side of such treatment. Maybe our behavior or our looks or our degree of knowledge (or lack thereof) has made us appear faulty or unimportant in someone else's eyes. Painful, isn't it? At those times it helps me to revisit my own thought patterns and make sure I'm thinking the kinds of honorable thoughts that make me thank God for everyone.

4. Think just thoughts—"right" (in the Greek, dikaia*).* Christian thought is intended to be free from bigotry and prejudice. We are to think rightly and justly about all situations, giving everyone the same chance in our consideration of them. In the process, we must evaluate every claim to Godlike thought on the basis of whether it helps us achieve that balance.

Churches that heal have pushed out bigotry and racism. There is no place in the Christian church for racial jokes, slurs, or attitudes of ethnic superiority. We must think correctly and righteously about God's call on humanity, which crosses every ethnic, cultural, age-related, and gender-based line we might try to draw.

5. *Think untainted thoughts—"pure" (in the Greek,* hagna). This thinking habit erases confusion, double-mindedness, and fruitless rumination. It basically says: Don't have two thoughts in one. Think about those things that are simple, trusted, and washed clean—things that encourage the fruit of the Spirit and not the flesh. God is purely in view when we think his pure thoughts.

6. *Have an eye for the beauty around you—"lovely" (in the Greek,* prosphile). This means we're to see the artistic side of life and not just be stuck on the pragmatic side. Too often, we evaluate things or think about people simply in terms of numbers or categories. But if we develop a habit of "lovely thinking," we will stand constantly amazed at the wonder of God's creation and the miraculous nature of the individual human spirit.

According to this passage in Philippians, believers are called to have a way of thinking about the world that is distinctly Christian. I like to think of it as seeing the world not with rose-colored glasses but with blood-red-colored glasses. When we think properly, we see differently. But it takes discipline to see as God sees. When the church can say with Jesus, "I only do what I see my Father doing" (see John 5:19), we can become a true healing environment.

THE POWER OF WORDS

Thought patterns, whether sound or unsound, eventually move on to speech. We can tell how people think by what they say. Stand in your church foyer sometime and listen to how people talk; it will tell you a great deal. In fact, your church's vocabulary can determine its degree of health.

According to the Book of Proverbs, words can have a tremendous healing impact. Solomon wrote, "Reckless words pierce like a sword, but the tongue of the wise brings healing" (Proverbs 12:18). "The tongue that brings healing is a tree of life, but a deceitful tongue crushes the spirit" (Proverbs 15:4). If these verses describe the impact of one person's words, imagine the power of an entire congregation's words!

Our words are powerful. They can be like charcoal stoking the flames of God's love for one another, or they can be like a bucket of ice water dousing the last dying embers of mutual concern and appreciation.

I remember the prayer meetings in the first church I ever attended. I would leave week after week totally demoralized. Finally, I spoke to one of the leaders of our college group. "There must be something terribly wrong here," I said. "I feel almost sick when I leave the prayer meetings."

"What do you mean?" my friend asked.

"Well, it's like we're complaining to God," I said. "We just moan about one hopeless situation after another. Where's God in all this? Aren't we supposed to have hope when we pray?"

My friend chuckled. "You know," he said, "I think you've put your finger on a very serious thing. There is an imbalance here."

The next week at our college meeting, my friend preached a message on the need for thanks and praise. And at the next prayer time, he started us off with this charge: We could only voice as many prayer requests as there were praise reports. For everything that was going wrong and needed prayer, there had to be something that was going right and deserved praise—something that God was accomplishing in our lives or the lives of others.

What a terrific healing environment that prayer meeting became! No, we weren't Pollyannas; we certainly continued to hear about the tough side of life. But it was marvelous to have our hope ignited by stories of families being restored, unemployed workers finding jobs, and temptations being overcome.

I remember one miracle distinctly. One of the students who came from a poor family had gone to the counselor's office to talk about dropping out. When he arrived, the counselor told him all of his school fees had been paid by someone he didn't know. Man, did we explode with excitement and joy!

Churches that heal discipline their minds and tongues to speak in ways that encourage spiritual growth, not tear it down. But it's not easy! Unfortunately, in the setting of a congregation, the "real us" often comes out under the pressure of relationships.

When I revealed my manic-depressive illness to my congregation several years ago, there were some who—out of fear and ignorance, I suppose—began speaking against me behind my back, hurting and confusing the church. Many people stopped coming to church as a result of this. Words do tear people and churches down. Even healthy churches can fall into this pit rather easily.

So much could have been resolved if only those folks had had a genuine concern for truth and the willingness to approach me face to face, as the Bible requires. Watch out for good people who break biblical rules! And count on it: Until you've talked with a person directly, you don't know *anything* about them.

I counsel a lot of churches. Most are fairly large. You'd think I'd get used to it, but I'm still blown away by the almost cavalier manner in which destructive words are hurled at leaders or staff without a moment's thought. I'm also surprised at the number of times leaders write off staff or congregation members rather than approaching them in loving confrontation. Anyone who is afraid of loving confrontation will not be part of a healing ministry. Churches that allow backbiting, character assassination, and disrespect toward others will never become healing places.

I can sense the verbal "spirit" of a congregation within minutes of my arrival. I can discern when a congregation is in the process of dismembering its pastor word by word over some silly issue. I can also tell when a congregation has been trained in mind and heart not to be susceptible to such foolishness. These latter groups talk with optimism about the vision of their church. They offer testimonies of the healing that occurs there.

Of course, all churches go through tough times. But you can gauge the spiritual health and vitality of a congregation by the words they use to convey their thoughts. Churches that heal constantly give themselves to the discipline of right thinking and proper speech. They understand that their words create an environment that outlasts the momentary burst of sound waves into the air.

Jesus' half brother, James, didn't have a lot of confidence in our ability to use speech wisely. One of the chapters I try to read in a disciplined fashion is James 3. It warns those of us who speak publicly that we're going to be judged according to stricter standards, and one of the main points of evaluation will be whether we learned to discipline our speech.

According to James, we're sort of like horses, and taming our tongues is like bridling a wild bronco. We're also like ships, he says, and our tongues are powerful rudders, steering us toward calm or stormy seas. What marvelous word pictures!

As a resident of the state of Washington, which boasts beautiful green forests in virtually every direction, I'm particularly sensitive to the illustration in James 3:5–6: "Consider what a great forest is set on fire by a small spark. The tongue also is a fire, a world of evil among the parts of the body. It corrupts the whole person, sets the whole course of his life on fire, and is itself set on fire by hell."

Occasionally, our local newscasters will announce that embers left by a careless camper got picked up by the wind, caught fire in the treetops, and eventually burned down acres and acres of forest land. Or they'll tell us that some psychopath intentionally threw a firebomb out a car window into the trees, starting a massive fire that burned out of control for days.

Scary to think that our words can cause comparable damage, isn't it?

How much better to have tongues that heal, that build up. Tongues that say "thank you" to a preacher. Tongues that say, "The children's classes are wonderful" or, "I want to volunteer." Tongues that make commitments to give. Tongues that call the newest visitor "friend." Tongues that say, "You just got divorced? I went through that, and God restored me." These are the messages of the disciplined tongues of a healing church.

Preaching That Builds Optimism

People today *listen* much differently than they did when I began preaching. I wouldn't say preaching is more difficult now, but it is definitely an interesting task to convey truth to postmodern ears. Contemporary people have many traits that weren't present years ago.

The following list isn't scientific, but here are some of the differences I've noted between people today and people approximately thirty years ago:

- Today's listeners have a shorter attention span. They are attuned to the seven-minute length of evening television content between commercials.
- They are more skeptical and relativistic. Listeners today don't believe anything just because you say it's true, or even because God says it's true. They have to be convinced.
- Today's listeners are more multisensory. They respond to messages that include drama, variety in music, and multimedia presentations.
- They are more "into" music. In fact, music is a big factor in communication with both postwar generations, the baby boomers and the baby busters.
- Today's listeners are nonjoiners. Unlike their predecessors, they're generally unwilling to make commitments, and they rarely support institutions of any kind.
- Today's listeners are more lonely, and they crave relationships.
- They are more change-weary and more time-starved.
- Today's listeners are serious seekers. They're not willing to settle for anything less than solid truth.
- Today's listeners crave hope. They come to church to hear *good* news.

But do they hear good news? That is the question all of us who are leaders must ask ourselves. How much bad news can today's postmodern take and be healed?

Preaching today must be loaded with optimism. It was the late Dr. Norman Vincent Peale who first put his finger on this by stating there is power in "positive thinking." The Bible calls it hope. Hope focuses our thinking on the fact that God can do anything in our lives. Not only can he, but he wants to. Not only does he want to, but he *will!*

As we'll see later in this chapter, positive thinking—or better yet, true biblical hope—creates optimism that heals.

Different ages require different emphases in preaching. I've read the sermons and writings of Charles Finney, the nineteenth-century revivalist, and gleaned several stellar insights. Finney said that we must discover how the Bible's message can best be heard in each era. Revival is always happening, but we have to discover the means of the moment—the method that will most effectively allow our listeners to respond.

As Finney would no doubt agree, the method that worked for him in the early- to mid-1800s won't work for us in the twenty-first century. The gospel itself, of course, in changeless. But Finney's was an austere emphasis, aimed at people who went to church but didn't believe. He loved to tear the folks down with a little hellfire and brimstone. The culture was made up of strong-willed individuals and strong families—not the broken people and torn-up families we see today.

The postmodern heart has been shattered by the broken promises of the secular age. Rampant divorce has left the baby busters with a deep-seated sense of instability, and they feel anger toward their baby-boomer parents. Meanwhile, the dreams of the boomers have collapsed into the harsh reality of economic limitations. The false promises of drug-induced euphoria have slipped through their fingers like sand.

Characteristics of Positive Preaching

The generations of our time need to hear a message of hope. We will only reach the contemporary heart and mind if our preaching and teaching include the following traits:

We must emphasize good news. If we are presenting a report about the church budget crunch or the latest fallen leader or the ungodly state of modern politics, we are not preaching good news. People who are not regular churchgoers tell me again and again that they are put off by the negativity of the patter from the pulpit. They really don't care how badly the church budget is doing. And even if they did, we should be sensitive enough to know that that's not what they need to hear.

How would you evaluate your own preaching? Do you find yourself taking care of dirty laundry in public services? If so, you are detracting from a more positive healing environment in your congregation.

We must emphasize affirming news. These days, we who are parents are regularly told how bad we are at raising kids. As part of the American work force, we're informed how lazy we are compared to the Japanese. Again and again, we are critiqued, evaluated, and rejected. Contemporary people are fed up with that kind of communication. When they come to church, they want to be affirmed. They want to discover at least a couple of things they are doing *right*. They want to be given permission to entertain the almost unimaginable thought that if God was Abraham's friend, he could be *theirs* too.

Does your preaching affirm what people are doing right? Do you pause in your messages to affirm those who have done well in their areas of life and service? If not, you're missing a grand opportunity to develop the healing gifts of your church.

We must let people know they can make a new start. Postmoderns can expect to have up to five careers in their lifetime. They have a good chance of having more than one marriage. Many have squandered years in unwise living, and the consequences can require a new start now and again. Fortunately, God is well known for giving people the means and the opportunity to start all over in Christ.

Are you a possibility preacher? If I were your guest this week and I had recently suffered a major setback, would I feel like I could make a new start in your church?

Ultimately, people need to start fresh by being born again in Jesus Christ. As a pastor-evangelist, I'm particularly sensitive about this. Many people I've led to Christ have told me that they sat in their old church year after year, never once hearing that they could experience a new life through faith in Jesus.

Do you give people an opportunity each week to become a new creature in Christ? If you make that offer on a regular basis, I guarantee many will be healed.

A message of acceptance must underlie everything we say and do. People in this secular age live with an acute awareness of self-alienation. By this I mean they sense they aren't put together well; they're not in touch with themselves. In fact, more often than not, they are working against themselves. Because they *feel* rejected, they sabotage their own lives, setting up self-fulfilling prophesies that cause them to *be* rejected.

Rejection is a common experience in today's fast-moving world, where sexual experience so often replaces love, and the "quick fix" replaces any attempt to alter one's lifestyle in a disciplined way. Ours is a world where marriages are easily terminated, kids are shuttled between homes, and employees are laid off after giving the best years of their lives to the company. This compounding of rejection has created a crying thirst for acceptance.

In your preaching, do you tell people every week that they are accepted by God? Does your church reach out to show unconditional love and acceptance to visitors, as well as to one another? If so, you're headed down the right path to a healing church.

We must express transparency from the pulpit. A number of years ago I visited a camp-teaching event in Mount Herman, California, where my friend Jerry Cook was speaking. As I listened to him, I was amazed. He opened up his life with a degree of transparency I've rarely heard in a teacher. Many listeners were healed in their hearts that night.

When we present ourselves as overly perfected examples of Christian living, people's antennae—and their walls—immediately go up. We can't possibly be who we say we are!

But when we share our struggles, our failings, and our faith, people are healed. They can identify with a speaker who will say, "Hey, I am broken in places too. But God has walked with me and restored me, and he'll do the same for you."

Of course, the sharing of shortcomings must be done in a balanced way, but can you open your heart wisely? If so, you're likely to see many postmoderns healed through your preaching.

We must talk more about what we're "for" than what we're "against." I've noticed that certain topics, when overemphasized from the pulpit, can be counterproductive in the effort to heal postmodern people—abortion, divorce, end times, and giving, among others. Now, each of these subjects is very important and should be part of the church's curriculum. But in this age of tremendously broken people, these topics can be easily overdone.

I have found that until people learn to be receivers of God's grace, they cannot become givers. Until they strongly find Jesus in the present, his second coming is only a cop-out.

Until they know why they are pro-life, being against abortion isn't enough. Until they understand godly love, they see no reason to resist divorce.

Do you teach and preach what you are *for*, rather than what you are *against?* It's really just another side to the same coin. But it's the side that will get heard and assimilated today, and people will be healed.

We must tell people about people. People today want to hear about other people. In my own experience, I've found that the kind of preaching that heals is filled with stories of people who have been healed. Both biblical figures and historical figures make great models for listeners to identify with. As believers in the Incarnation, we shouldn't be surprised; God became man because he knew it would take talking about man from the heart of a man to touch and heal our deepest needs.

People in the postmodern generations don't care much about hermeneutics or word studies unless they can be included in a story about a person. People, people, people! Stories of people heal. That's why Christ's parables are such excellent teaching tools even today. Two thousand years later, his stories about people are still healing human hearts.

Do you teach like Jesus did, telling stories about people to make your points? Do you imagine that you will be talking to hurting and broken individuals when you prepare your messages? If not, you are missing a significant key to seeing healing happen in your church.

Healthy People in a Positive Church

It's true: A church that consciously pursues a healing environment by encouraging optimistic, hope-filled thinking will positively affect the physical health of its members. According to scientific studies, the body's T cells (the kind that drive the immune system) actually increase when optimistic thinking is applied. In a positive environment, the immune system works better, and overall health is improved.

In his book *Learned Optimism*, Dr. Martin Seligman concludes that a lack of optimism not only makes people feel bad emotionally, it can actually lead to poor physical health. Pessimism promotes depression; it produces inertia rather than activity in the face of a challenge or setback. It also has a tendency to be self-fulfilling, but when pessimists are right and things really do turn out badly, they only feel worse.

Perhaps you will be as interested as I was in the following study of healthy and sick lawyers related by Dr. Howard Friedman in his book *The Self-Healing Personality: Why Some People Achieve Health and Others Succumb to Illness*.

> Lawyers face many challenges in their work—their duties are by definition adversarial, and the pace is fast. As part of a larger program of research, we happened to study two lawyers—one who was ill and one who was healthy. We found some suggestive differences. The ill lawyer, who was fighting disease, although pleasant on the surface, was extremely suspicious and almost

> became paranoid and combative about answering questions. The healthy attorney was very busy but exuded a sense of confidence and self-control. Interestingly, these impressions have been confirmed in two large studies of lawyers.
>
> The first study involved 128 lawyers who initially were examined when they were in law school in the 1950s. At that time, they were administered a psychological test.... Of special interest were subscales that measured cynicism, hostile feelings, and aggressive tendencies—the choleric personality.
>
> By 1985, thirteen of the lawyers (10 percent) in this study had died. As might be expected from population statistics, the deaths were due to heart disease, cancer, and diabetes. Was the mortality related to personality? The results clearly show that the higher one's choleric tendencies, the greater the risk of dying within the thirty-year period. In fact, the lawyers who scored at around the seventy-fifth percentile were about five times as likely to die as those who scored around the twenty-fifth percentile.[1]

To use our own terms, the lawyers who retained a positive, confident, optimistic outlook fared better healthwise than those who were moody and pessimistic. I'm all the more convinced that churches that devote themselves to maintaining an atmosphere of biblical hope and optimism will create an environment that is conducive to physical health and every other kind of health.

It is an extraordinary power we have as preachers, and one we rarely think about: Through our words and demeanor, we can actually affect the neurological systems of the people in our congregation, for

1. Howard S. Friedman, *The Self-Healing Personality: Why Some People Achieve Health and Others Succumb to Illness* (New York: Henry Holt and Company, 1991), 103–4.

better or worse. The very cells of our bodies can be impacted by the messages we speak in our services.

Churches that heal see hope as the primary focus of every service—not hope in oneself, not hope in the economy, not hope in the government, but hope in Christ Jesus. Jesus is the object of our hope, and when he is applied like a balm to our hurting hearts, healing occurs.

Every time history repeats itself,
the price goes up.

Ralph Waldo Emerson

12

Contending for Reality

Karl Marx claimed that religion was "the opiate of the people." And for about seventy years, Russians were encouraged to look down on believers as weak people in need of a crutch.

Unfortunately, you don't have to share your faith very long before you find out that people in America tend to agree with Marx—not everyone, but the majority. They say, "Whatever makes you feel alive, believe it" or, "If that's your thing, then do it." It's almost as if religion is just a fairy tale or a fiction novel.

And frankly, many of our churches and theologies have been guilty of promoting spiritual "alternate realities"—fantastical views of the world that don't have the remotest connection with everyday life.

For years, in poll after poll, unchurched people have said that they would attend church if they thought it was going to have some pragmatic value for their daily living.

As it is, they view Christianity as a set of axioms that apply to a realm with no visible connection to life in the real world.

Can our faith be connected to reality and still be biblical? Certainly; in fact, having a strong connection with reality is an important part of being a healing church.

HOW CHURCHES CREATE ALTERNATE REALITIES

When it comes to healing, there are some deadly theologies that have made the rounds among churches in this country. Groups have been taught that if they "confess" properly, avoid doctors, ignore their symptoms, and *act* like they're healed, they will be healed.

That's a fantasy belief. A *biblical* faith is one that networks with all that is true, sound, and healthy, whatever the field. Faith sees God in any act of healing that does not defame his name.

I know I've spotted fantasy faith when I hear of people who will not go to a psychologist for marriage counseling, even though a professional would be able to offer sound advice on how to improve communication with their spouses. I suspect fantasy faith when adult children of alcoholic parents will not consider a twelve-step program to help them understand certain recurring emotional difficulties in their lives. I know it's fantasy faith when I hear individuals boast about their refusal to take perscription medicine for a serious health problem.

The Bible says to test all things (see 1 Thessalonians 5:21). Test them to see if they are of God. If they aren't prohibited in the Bible; if they lead to health; and if they either glorify God or at least do not detract from God, then they ought to be considered as part of our arsenal for healing. Staying away from doctors, counselors, or other healing professionals or networks does not exhibit our faith; rather, it exhibits our stupidity.

My own bipolar disorder is well under control through effective treatment. Because I've been willing to talk about it, I get a high number of calls from Christians confused about this topic. I remember one in particular.

Eileen, the mother of two teenagers, called me about her seventeen-year-old daughter, Kristin. Kristin was in deep depression, but at times she had surges of energy and creativity that pushed her out of control. In recent weeks she had withdrawn from her family, and her grades had taken such a drastic plunge that she was in danger of not graduating from high school.

Even though the family did not attend my church, I invited the two to come to my office. I took Kristin through the standard checklist of depression symptoms.

"Have you seen a doctor about your moods?" I asked her. "You match most of the traits of a person with bipolar disorder, which is also called manic-depression. I am bipolar, so I know what it's like. You need to have your doctor check this out." I paused, then added, "By the way, did your father ever have mood swings?"

Her mother spoke up. "Her father was my second husband. He died when Kristin was seven. He definitely was a wild man. He could be great fun, but he was a daredevil too. He died trying to rescue some kids off the side of a cliff. He had a drinking problem, and I think that may be the reason he fell." She began to cry softly.

"Have you had any depression, Eileen?" I asked.

"Only when it would be appropriate, I think," she said, wiping her tears. "But besides my husband, Kristin has an uncle who committed suicide. I'm really frightened for my daughter."

"Don't worry, Mom," Kristin said, patting her mother's arm. Then she turned to me. "I'm trusting God to take care of me, Pastor," she said unemotionally. "I'm part of the youth group at my church, and my pastor believes this is a spiritual problem. He says that God can heal me. Our church doesn't believe in going to doctors."

"Gee, are you sure that's what they believe?" I asked.

"Yes," she said somewhat sternly. "And they warned me about you and your church because you have a weak faith and have led people the wrong way."

"Well, I'll tell you, Kristin, that's a dangerous belief. If you'd like, I'd be willing to talk to your pastor and see if we can't impress on him how serious your situation is."

"I don't think we need to," she said, then stopped. Her voice softened. "Do you think I'm in danger?"

"Yes, I think you are in danger. At the very least, I know you are miserable. I've been there, done that," I said. "I think this group you are part of *sounds* religious, but their advice to you is not biblical or wise. How 'bout I take you to a doctor I know who works with teenagers who are bipolar or depressed, and then you decide what you think?"

As it turned out, Kristin got some great help. Within weeks of taking the proper medication, she had come out of her depression and was getting As and Bs in school. And over the next six months, about six of her friends, along with her mom and stepdad, started coming to our church.

There is an opposite to fantasy faith—a counterfantasy, if you will. That is the fantasy of secularism. Secularism says that our world is a "closed system" in which there are no dimensions beyond what we can see, hear, and touch. Only this mundane world is real. In such a system, God does not intervene.

Of course, those of us who are devoted to the Scriptures know that there is a spiritual realm that is just as much a reality as the physical world. And just as the fields of science have proven that our physical world doesn't run on guesswork but on sound laws (such as the law of gravity), so the spiritual realm is not a matter of guesswork but of solid, sensible, godly principles.

Churches that heal poke holes in the non-realities of religious systems as well as the counterfantasies of the secular, humanistic worldview. God's world, and the world of the church, is an "open creation" that is also extremely pragmatic and wise.

How to Break Myths about Faith

I've found that people in life transitions often exhibit a kind of chronic uneasiness. Women in their midthirties sometimes go through a crisis of identity and become very uneasy about their lives. Men in their forties can experience the same thing. People get itchy. Values change. Goals get tossed aside.

These are dangerous times for folks who are spiritually sensitive but not grounded in reality. Such personality types are prone to making sweeping changes much too quickly. Perhaps after spending half a lifetime playing a "safe" faith, they go off the deep end and sell everything to run a youth camp in the Andes. Or after working with a company for two decades, they quit eighteen months short of drawing retirement in order to start a little church on a street corner. The uneasiness people feel when they realize that they've not gotten from life what they thought they would or have not done for God what they thought they should can prompt some pretty drastic responses.

God is sensible and makes sense, and he encourages us to behave sensibly.

Sometimes in our attempts to help people, however, we in the church promote myths instead of reality. For example, we tell a man and woman who are having marital problems that if they just give their lives to Christ, their marriage will become heavenly overnight. Granted, there is a dramatic change that takes place when we experience the forgiveness of Christ, and it does have a way of jarring every area of our life in a strong way. Yet many couples who get born again with the hope that they'll always have a happy marriage eventually find that the same habits that caused problems before they met Christ are still causing problems. And what do they do then? The fantastical promises of a faulty faith can deal a disillusioning blow.

Another myth is that when someone really gets converted, they are able to stop all addictions at once. Wrong. I have found that converts to Christ have a longer-lasting sobriety than those who try to go at it without God. But short term, Christian or not, about 85 percent of people who struggle with addictions relapse in the first two years. Unfortunately, Christians sometimes resist going back to the church for help because they've been told their relapses mean they've left Christ. This may or may not be true. What is true is that they have gotten off track and need help in returning to a healthy path.

Here's another one: Christians are supposed to be the happiest people in the world. It's automatic, right? As with the other myths, there are some problems inherent in this notion. One, the Bible talks a lot about our being sad and even mourning because of our faith. Two, we are commanded to be joyful, but joy is not the same as happiness; it's much deeper. Joylessness may be deadly for a believer, but there is nothing wrong, biblically speaking, with being unhappy.

Any number of medical or emotional conditions will give you depression. Abuse, rejection, or loss will make you sad. You can suffer from any of these and still be a Christian. But too often we treat someone who is depressed as if they've also lost their faith! Sad, isn't it?

Proactive Steps to Biblical Spirituality

Churches that heal reject spiritual fantasies that seep into our theologies in the name of faith. They also take proactive measures to build reality-based, biblical spirituality in their people. Following are five steps I always recommend.

1. *Prescribe five chapters a day.* When someone comes to me for healing, I tell them to do this simple thing: Read the Bible. "Five chapters a day will keep the pastor away," I joke. I assure them that in reading and meditating on the Word, they will find the full release of healing and understanding in their situation. The Book of Proverbs is a particularly pointed source of wisdom for those wrestling with fantasies.

2. *Confront people without laying on a guilt trip.* When we confront a person, we should never bark, "I think you are believing fantasies" or, "You are out of touch with reality." Healthy confrontation is not disrespectful or superior in tone; it doesn't judge in a way that closes the other's ears. It does not inflict guilt. Rather, it invites dialogue and often begins with a question.

For example, we might ask gently, "Do you think what you're doing is healthy?" The other person may open up enough to respond, "Well, I have felt a little uneasy." The key is that this person must sense that even if he doesn't agree with you, you'll still love him.

Galatians 6:1 is our pattern. We're to correct a brother and help him get back on track with a spirit of gentleness and kindness.

Most leaders run into alternate realities often. I spent three months trying to avoid a woman who was sure that she was called by God to lead the queen of England to Christ. I mean, what do you do? Do you want to squelch such an ambition if it could possibly be from God? Things got a little ridiculous, however, when she started claiming that former Vice President Dan Quayle was going to help her get in to see the queen. My wife and I doubted that.

Unfortunately, this woman's husband was also caught up in the fantasy. I finally felt such pain for them that I knew I had to confront them and bring them into reality. I started by saying, "Helen and Jim, I've talked to you several times about my concern that you check out the validity of some of your claims to a calling. They sound a bit grandiose to me. I would encourage some counseling and also a medical checkup for Helen."

Angry, Helen blurted out, "What do you know? You're not such a great pastor, after all."

I held my ground. "I love you guys," I said, "but this is not Christianity. This is a fantasy. You don't have to do big things for God; he just wants little things done well. Somewhere along the way, in my opinion, something in your lives hasn't been healed, and you haven't been able to accept yourselves as you are. God has accepted you. I accept you. But this fantasy is destroying you, and I encourage you to break out of it."

"We knew you wouldn't appreciate our calling," Helen said. "You're just jealous about it, like all our other pastors have been."

At that point, Jim interrupted her. I think he sensed that I really did care. "The Bible *does* say that we are to respect those who are over us in the Lord, Helen. And if Pastor Doug says we need to question this, I'm going to question it. Maybe you *aren't* well."

Eventually it was discovered that, in fact, Helen suffered from an emotional disorder that led her to have surges of grandiose thoughts followed by severe collapses into depression. Slowly but surely, through treatment and sound biblical teaching, she and Jim found their way back to a reality-based faith in Christ.

3. *Get people into small groups.* Many of the people that come to Christ in our churches today need to be healed in a number of practical, tangible ways. For instance, large numbers have lived with unrealistic ideas about money—how to get it, how to spend it, how God thinks about financial blessing—and they have high levels of debt and stress as a result.

I once counseled a young man in his late twenties who had run up an American Express bill to more than twenty thousand dollars. He had gotten overly optimistic about a business prospect.

Having had numerous successes before, he was certain that this one would work out well too. But it didn't. When he came to my office to commit his life to Christ, he pleaded with me, "How can I deal with this debt?"

"As you give your life to Christ, do you believe he's going to get rid of this debt for you?" I asked him.

"Isn't that what he promises?"

"No, actually, he does not," I said. "He tells us to live within our means and to be responsible for our debts. I believe God is going to build your character by teaching you to pay off this debt one day at a time."

He looked disappointed. The Christianity he'd heard about from friends and television preachers presented a God who is something like a heavenly butler. When you snap your fingers, he solves all of your problems.

It's frightening to think how prevalent this view of God has become in this country. No doubt everyone reading this book has been influenced by it to some degree. But God is not our butler. We are his creatures. He is the Lord, and we are his slaves. God's main goal for us is not that we'll have a *comfortable* life; his goal is that we'll live a *God-honoring* life.

We need to state this over and over again as we lead new people to Christ. But I have come to believe that, more often than not, we leaders really can't help people make major character changes or break down long-held fantasies from our place in the pulpit.

We may inspire them to want to change. We may give them spiritual principles that will bear fruit in conjunction with a more personal approach. But I'm convinced that the best context for learning to live in reality is in a small group. That's where real change is most likely to occur—where people can interact on a personal level and accountability is possible.

When dealing with myths about money, special classes can help as well. In such settings, teaching can be specific and interaction can be personal. I also recommend that churches train a team of people, or even several teams, who can offer practical, one-on-one assistance to people coming out of financial bondage.

4. Teach people to accept the consequences. When I finished my last pastorate, I decided I would analyze my preaching topics and evaluate how well I'd done as a teacher with the same congregation for more than fifteen years. In spite of what the congregation's opinion might have been, I thought I was near-genius! But there were so many glaring imbalances—so many things I should have talked about, but didn't—that I could only ask God to forgive me.

One of the things I must have been uncomfortable talking about was consequences. I preached few sermons instructing people how to bear up responsibly in the aftermath of their bad choices or faulty thinking. But I've come to believe that healing churches must teach people how to live with the consequences of their sins and false belief systems while at the same time encouraging them to believe in the miraculous touch of God. This is not an easy assignment, but it is important.

There are consequences to our actions, whether we're Christians or not! I can't tell you the number of couples I've sat and cried with who, after coming to Christ in their later years, couldn't understand why God didn't heal their kids now too. I've counseled many people guilty of crimes who, after accepting Christ, couldn't fathom why they were still sent to prison by a court of law.

The answer is simple: It's the law of consequences. It's the law of sowing and reaping. Churches that contend for reality accept the fact that there are real consequences that befall our misdeeds. We must embrace those consequences and thank God for them, knowing that looking them in the eye can only make us better people.

How naive I used to be, sitting in marriage counseling sessions where one spouse had been unfaithful and praying that God would heal the marriage instantly and save the couple from all the fallout of the indiscretion! The fact is, when an affair occurs, trust is broken, and emotions such as anger and resentment must be dealt with—not shuffled under a table of religious-sounding fantasy. Over time I've learned that couples end up with better relationships and more complete healing when they actually face the issues that fostered the infidelity.

We're better off preaching that God will help us walk through the consequences we are sure to face from misbehavior than encouraging people to expect an instant "fix" in messy situations. And somewhere along the way, we must mention the idea of restitution. It's a ticklish subject, but I believe restitution—paying back or otherwise rectifying the damage caused by our sin—is the often-overlooked flip side of repentance.

We shouldn't approach restitution, however, as "one size fits all." One of my friends was a habitual criminal. He spent twenty of his first thirty years as a felon before coming to Christ and turning his life around. I noticed him one time sitting on the back row while I was teaching a class on biblical restitution to a group of college students.

After the class, he said to me, "Whew! I'm going to need about five years off."

"Why?" I asked.

"It's going to take me that long to make restitution."

I realized then that we, as leaders, must apply great wisdom when it comes to recommending steps of restitution to broken people who've left long, messy trails. Nevertheless, I believe most of us would experience deeper healing and a greater heart-cleansing if we were encouraged to repay and restore the people we've hurt.

5. *Be firm—and loving.* I have learned that there are two mistakes we can make when we try to help people who struggle with addictions, mental ailments, or even faulty beliefs. We can fail to confront them, choosing to support and "enable" their behavior in the name of love, or we can bark instructions and make vacuous threats in an attempt to control them. If we're not too experienced, we may jump from one extreme to the other.

People who are bringing destruction upon themselves need to be approached firmly and decisively. But even more, they need to be treated with love and respect. And if they're the ones who've taken the step to reach out to us for help, they don't need information or advice as much as they just need *us*.

I can be a determined and forceful helper in such cases. But I have also learned that I must let the person know that they have my heart—no matter what.

I once tried to help an NBA superstar beat his cocaine addiction. The courts placed him under my custody, making me responsible, essentially, for anything he did. I knew my first task was to convince him that he'd never have a better friend than me and that I was more committed to *him* than to getting him to stay *clean*.

One afternoon I walked into his room and could smell cocaine. He freebased the stuff, which means he vaporized it and inhaled it through a pipe.

"What is this?" I asked as I scooped up some white powder from the window ledge.

"I don't know—maybe some chalk from my socks," he said, trying his best to look honest. But his facial expression betrayed him.

"You're a lousy liar," I said. "You know I love you, and you have a choice now. We can lock up all your money and credit cards in a safe. I'll have the only key. We can get someone to take inventory so you don't have to worry about me stealing anything. Then I can take you back to the clinic, park your car in your wife's garage, and keep the keys.

"Or I can go to the telephone and call the judge. I can tell her that I gave you one chance and you blew it and now you want to go to jail for eighteen months. It's your choice."

"I won't do it again. Honest, man, don't take my car," he begged.

"Nope," I responded, "you only had one chance with me, and I told you that on day one. You're not going to push me around, and that's it." I stopped and headed for the phone.

"Okay, man, let's go to the clinic. I'll get my stuff."

My friend, after a few falls, made it. He beat the addiction. And he knows I love him to this day.

Churches that heal don't play games with God or others. They don't give place to fantasies—even religious-sounding ones that fail to line up with Scripture, proven human experience, or the laws of wisdom. If we want to be a community that brings true, lasting healing to the people around us, we must contend for reality.

No man is an island intire of it selfe; every man in a peece of the Continent, a part of the maine; if a Clod bee washed away by the Sea, Europe is the lesse, as well as if a Promontorie were; As well man's death diminishes me, because I am involved in Mankinde; and therefore never send to know for whom the bell tolls; It tolls for thee.

John Donne

13

Walking in Another's Moccasins

I'm no connoisseur, but I do enjoy an occasional walk through an art museum. I've noticed that in the really great paintings—the Gauguins or the Rembrandts or the van Goghs—I'm usually drawn to one thing, like a dominant color or a facial feature that makes the whole picture come alive for me. Without that element, there's nothing to look at.

That's what *compassion* is to healing. It isn't just *part* of the picture of restoring lives. Compassion is all of the picture.

To be compassionate is to be moved in our guts, to mysteriously experience another's pain. It is to listen, to hear the other person's side of the story before we speak, to understand. It's what makes healing come alive.

In our contemporary world, large numbers of people need healing from addictions and mood disorders. These are the great plagues of our time. But too often, the church is the worst place for an alcoholic, a drug addict, an anorexic, or a depressed person to go for help. The simple reason is we don't listen with compassion. But we'll never heal anyone if we don't learn to listen with our hearts.

The caricature attached to preaching is somewhat dismaying. I have often had someone respond, "Now you're *preaching* at me," when I have simply been trying to tell them how they could improve. Preaching has a negative stigma, I think, because it implies speaking without listening. We all know that this is the number one cause of problems in marriage (and other areas of life). If either partner feels they are not being listened to, compassion and respect break down.

This is the crux of the matter: You cannot heal someone you don't respect.

Standing for truth in the midst of broken lives does not mean annihilating the ones we're trying to help. I've been part of attempts to help people that were more harmful than their difficulties were. A dear friend of mine died because the radiation shot into his body to defeat a tumor actually killed his liver. This is what we Christians are often guilty of.

There is many a hapless saint who has been radiated to death by the gospel-truth gun. I remember one family that just couldn't leave their nineteen-year-old daughter alone. Mom, dad, older brother, aunts, uncles—the entire family turned preacher when she was around. I honestly felt sorry for her.

It was clear she didn't like her parents' brand of faith. And since she was nineteen, what was anyone going to do about it? She didn't have enough money to move out, and her parents had promised her tuition money if she stayed at home.

This was one of those situations I was able to take care of over the pastor's trusty cell phone on the golf course. My secretary, Vivian, called me to let me know that one of the office staffers had been intimidated into giving the mother my cell phone number.

I continued to play—I was even winning for a change—when the call came on the eleventh hole.

"Hello, is this Pastor Doug?" a high, excited voice asked as soon as I flipped the little mouthpiece back.

"Yes, is this Claudia?" I asked.

"That's right. Pastor, you have to head over here immediately," she blurted out. "We're beside ourselves. Cindy didn't come in until 3:30 A.M., and she has a non-Christian boyfriend. Who knows what happened. We need your help right away."

"Now, Claudia," I said, "I can't come over today. I have something I am doing. Why are you surprised that Cindy has a non-Christian boyfriend? She isn't a Christian." I stopped and braced myself for the explosion.

"She is so! We all have given her Bible verse after Bible verse. She just isn't growing in the Lord. She did better with the old youth pastor," she fired back, hardly coming up for air.

"Cindy is too old for the youth group now. She is an adult. And she doesn't want to be a Christian, so let her not be one. Can you hear what I am saying?"

"The Bible says we are to confront and admonish one another in the faith. I bet you wouldn't be so relaxed if this were your child!" she fumed.

"Well, as a matter of fact, I have a child I love very much who is just like Cindy—twenty-one years old and not interested in Christianity right now. And you know, I wouldn't mind having Cindy as a daughter. I think she is very honest."

"Okay," Claudia said. "If you're not coming over and you are so smart, what do you think we should do?"

"I think you guys have driven her nuts with all the Bible thumping. You are telling her she is too stupid to hear God on her own. I understand it's likely she's doing things none of us would approve of. But what she needs is for the whole bunch of you to shut up and respect her as she lives her life.

"Set some rules. That's fair; she is under your roof, after all. But for Jesus' sake, leave the Bible out of it. Just love and respect her. And shut up. Make no comment about her friends or her appearance. She will be so shocked she just might find faith again.

"Trust the Holy Spirit. If she asks, 'What happened to the Bible patrol?' just tell her she has to live her own life."

"But, Pastor, you don't understand. She's even dyed her hair green!"

"Okay," I said.

"What do you mean, okay? Would let your daughter have green hair?"

"Well, you know, I think it looks pretty cool. Cindy just wants to be herself and not you. It's called 'healthy differentiation.' She will get worse the more you push her, trust me," I concluded.

"Well, I will discuss this with my husband," she said with resignation. "Sorry for interrupting your meeting."

"Call again if you want," I answered, and we hung up.

It was my turn at the tee. I went for a perfect fade to the left, but the ball hooked right and slammed into the side of a house off the fairway.

Cindy did eventually come to Christ, green hair and all. She even married one of the sons of a staff pastor about four years later. No green hair that day!

There is such a thing as giving people too much truth. A healing church will attract a high number of people who struggle with sexual sin, divorce, addictions, and mental or emotional illness. But legalism or "hyper-Bible" therapy is no cure for these issues. Instead, we must learn to trust the Holy Spirit's work in the lives of others. Only the Holy Spirit can transform a life.

Helping the Addicted

What is an addiction? Simply, it's a habituation to a chemical, practice, or even a person that keeps you from functioning in wholeness and that cannot be broken without help. People may become addicted to cocaine, Xanax, marijuana, sex, pornography, shopping, self-mutilation, voyeurism, another person (someone they are drawn to even though they cannot righteously have him or her), and even plastic surgery. Any repeated behavior that just has to be done fits the definition.

It's a tricky thing to reach people caught in addictive patterns. They don't want to be preached at. It takes a great deal of energy and understanding to let them know we're just *there*, available, ready to listen with a compassionate heart.

I believe one of the primary ways we can let people know we are listening is to educate ourselves about the issues they are facing. We can learn to apply Scripture in effective ways that express our compassion. We can also make visible demonstrations of concern and care—for example, developing Alcoholics Anonymous or other support groups in our churches.

When we demonstrate that we are listening, that we really care, they will come; and with addiction running rampant throughout our society, there are a lot of "them." In fact, a lot of "them" are "us." A doctor friend of mine estimates that nearly 20 percent of the people sitting in our church auditoriums each week are predisposed to alcoholism alone. The way sugar is digested in their bodies sets them up to be addicted more quickly and much more thoroughly than the other 80 percent of the population.

Some refer to alcoholism as a disease. I would not want to argue with the medical community, but I would say it is a disease and more. Physiology, psychology, and spiritual illness are all factors.

During my last month as pastor of Eastside Church, I gave an entire morning to the subject of alcohol addiction. I explained that I wanted to talk to all the Christians who had alcohol problems and to explain how they could get free. "But first," I said, "I want to tell you what I know about alcoholism." It made a great message. One hundred nineteen people out of about thirty-three hundred adults in attendance immediately sought help after the service. About a fifth actually got involved in small groups to help defeat this bondage in their lives.

WHY OUR EFFORTS FAIL

Unfortunately, most churches have dismal records when it comes to helping addicted people. Let's look at three of the main reasons.

1. *We tend to rely too heavily on ascribing a moral solution for everything.* You know, Jesus didn't operate this way. When his disciples asked him in John 9:2 who had sinned to cause a man's blindness, Jesus rejected the moralist theory. "It's for the glory of God," he told them. I think Jesus was saying, "Hello? That's irrelevant to the situation here. Just step back and watch. I'm going to heal this man!"

2. *We often have little patience for the relapses that all addicts face.* As we mentioned in the last chapter, about 85 percent of recovering

addicts will relapse in their first two years. In churches, we often refer to these people as "backsliders" and assume that they have chosen to walk away from God's grace. The fact is, we *all* slip at times because of weakness. An addict's relapses are just more obvious. Of course, we shouldn't be apathetic about relapses back into addiction. We know that addiction kills. But we must be committed to the person more than to our idea of acceptable progress. Just being there—not appalled, not condemning, but just there, listening—may be the very thing that brings them back to wholeness. It's the Galatians 6:1 principle again.

I know it can be frustrating to deal with addicts. At one point at Eastside, it became apparent that we were attracting more addiction-oriented disorders than we could handle.

We just didn't have enough pastors to deal with the numbers. Then we decided—long before twelve-step groups were popular in churches—that the best person to help an addict was a recovered addict. We began our first support group, then asked people who'd been helped toward health to bring others. They led the new people to Christ, and more addicts began to be healed.

This worked amazingly well. It became clear that someone who has been freed from addiction has a great deal more patience with addicts than someone who doesn't understand the forces of an addictive pattern.

Galatians 4:4 gives us an interesting understanding of how a ministry relates to its time. Paul said that at the perfect or appointed time, God sent his Son into the world. I believe twelve-step ministries to broken and addicted people are not just fads; they are a greatly needed ministry at this time in history.

3. *We tend not to let people grow.* This is one of the saddest aspects of church life. We Christians are not very good at letting people grow to be who they are meant to be in the Lord Jesus Christ. We lock people into old identities or our own ideas of who they are or should be. Parents don't let their children forget the mistakes of their youth. Former addicts are watched with eagle eyes for signs of failure.

As I read the Book, it says that we died and are now alive in Christ. This means that we are now identified with Jesus and are leading his life. From day to day the Holy Spirit is transforming us into someone more closely aligned with the person God created us to be. We're changing from "glory to glory," as it says in 2 Corinthians 3:18 (KJV).

I've asserted this before: A serious epidemic of memory loss would help the church of Jesus Christ a great deal. If we could forget who people were and rejoice in who they *are*, we could be much more effective in helping the addicted move toward fullness of health in Christ. In a church environment where addicts aren't expected to act like addicts anymore, healing occurs.

Helping the Depressed

I'm convinced the majority of churches today understand very little about depression. Most of us still hold to common mistaken notions about depressed people: They're weak; they don't read the Bible enough; they have some secret sin; they were abused as children.

It is certain that all of these things can contribute to a cycle of depression. But we can't be a helper or healer for someone struggling with depression if we're looking for an easy answer.

It is critical that the church learn more about depression and discover how to network with other professionals and groups to heal depressed people. I once asked an eminent psychiatrist, Dr. Raymond Vath, how many churchgoing people he thought were depressed. His answer sobered me.

"Well, Doug, there are a number of factors to consider," he stated. "We know that pastors and ministers of churches are often the very first ones that depressed people go to for help, even though churches as a whole have very little understanding about how to heal depression. We also know that a church tends to be a close sampling of the community it serves and that 20 percent of Americans are predisposed—either genetically or through life events in early childhood—to clinical depression.

"Add that all up, and it is my personal belief that 30 percent of any congregation is likely to be in a depressive episode of one sort or another."

When I heard this statement, it gave me great pause. It means that whenever I step up to the podium as a speaker or worship leader, I am ministering before a group in which nearly one out of every three is probably depressed! One-third are struggling to feel connected to the church or to anyone or anything else. Some are probably suicidal, and God has brought them there.

I've learned to acknowledge the fact that there are people sitting in the sanctuary who, due to their depression, cannot feel a part of what is happening. To ask them to act happy, to rejoice and clap their hands, can actually be cruel. People in such a state need to be given permission to simply receive and let the presence of the joy of the Lord heal their hearts and minds.

As with addictions, we can show we care by becoming informed. Depression certainly matches the normal definition we give to it of "melancholy" or "despair," but there are a number of specific symptoms that we can check for when we interview people we suspect are depressed, such as insomnia, irritability, intestinal upset, relational conflicts, low self-esteem, lethargy, a pervasive sense of sadness or hopelessness, and thoughts of suicide.

Of course, some depression is only normal and human—those feelings any of us would experience at the death of a loved one, for example. It would be a remarkably ill person who didn't feel grief and some depression after such a loss! But taking a person through a checklist can be a tip-off that, either through situational pressures or genetics, depression may be at work.

I have found in my ministry that many life problems can be directly related to the presence of depression. It is often one of the culprits in extramarital affairs. When a man or a woman becomes depressed, they typically feel a sense of not connecting with their spouse or with God, and they may seek this connection with someone else who sparks a certain "chemistry." I've found again and again that when the depression is dealt with first, other issues underlying the infidelity come to light, and the recovery is remarkable.

There is a specific form of depression that is important to mention here: bipolar disorder or manic-depression. Bipolar illness is characterized by mood swings in which an individual, due to a chemical imbalance in the brain, swings from hyperactivity and a high sense of ecstasy to severe depression and melancholy. Both it and the more common "unipolar" depression can lead to *psychosis*—a separation from reality that can make a person delusional, schizophrenic, or paranoid.

The good news is that both unipolar and bipolar depression can be treated. My own bipolar disorder has been under control for years now through not only effective medical treatment but also spiritual discipline and the grace of God. I sought help when I realized that some of my symptoms were very clearly wearing out the people around me, especially my wife. I was keeping a manic pace. In pastoral situations that required confrontation, I was very impulsive. I was also having extraordinary difficulty sleeping.

In my traveling and speaking, the adrenaline would kick in when I was in front of a congregation or seminar audience, and I wouldn't be able to sleep for several days in a row. If I had another engagement scheduled right afterward, I could end up going seven to ten days without sleep. Sometimes I would be up late imploring, "Please, God, just let me get some rest." Upon my return home, depression would hit. I would sit in my darkened room reading my Bible, sequestered from everyone.

I shared the story of my struggle with my congregation, against the advice of a number of people who were concerned about the reaction I'd get. And certainly, the outcome was not all positive. Still, I believe I did the right thing. Since bringing the illness into the open, I've been sought out by hundreds of people, including numerous doctors and pastors, who've wanted to discuss their own depression or mood disorder. And I've been able to network with others to make sure that each one got the help they needed.

Over and over again I've been told, "For the first time, I know that somebody understands what I've been dealing with. I know I can trust you because you understand what I'm feeling."

That is exactly the point. The first and best thing a church can do for a person with a mood disorder is to become educated, offer understanding, and then follow through with compassion.

A church can also network with experts. Even though I am personally very familiar with the subject of depression, I recognize that I am not qualified to help very many people. Churches that heal the depressed must network with psychiatric hospitals, Christian psychologists, and others trained to deal with the medical issues involved.

I advise pastors not to try to do long-term pastoral counseling with people suffering from serious depression, psychosis, or bipolar disorder. Trust me: It will wear you out. We must set strong boundaries around the extent of care we can bring to such an individual and then direct them to the appropriate professionals who can treat them.

With a limited amount of research, a church can locate Christian doctors, psychologists, and other professionals who are willing to help. We need them. And the fact is, pastors have many insights in this area that doctors need to hear. Most M.D.s don't understand how guilt can exacerbate the core issues in depression and how redemption answers the issue of guilt.

I invite a group of medical doctors, psychiatrists, and psychologists once or twice a year to a lunch to exchange information and develop relationships. At the meeting, I arrange for a Christian doctor or other professional to teach on some aspect of depression or new drug therapy. Pastors are included, and they always ask a lot of questions. We close the time talking about how we can do a better job networking with one another. And it has truly become a two-way exchange: Many of the professionals now refer people to our church when they realize they're dealing with spiritual issues.

A church can also help people who have mood disorders by networking them with other people in the congregation. Just as we've found that the best person to help a drug addict is a recovered drug addict, the best person to help someone who is depressed is another person who has struggled through the same condition and learned to control it.

Years ago, I had a local Christian psychiatrist speak in our service, describing the spiritual, medical, dietary, and emotional aspects of depression. After his message, we invited people who had dealt with depression to help us develop a team that would offer care to others. The response was tremendous. We had folks who had suffered on many different levels express their willingness to get involved. Eventually, a local psychologist and his wife volunteered to lead the whole program. As a result, I have seen many hopeless people come to wholeness.

Why Is Depression So Misunderstood?

Not all depression is bad, as we've noted. It's something like a fever: A fever can actually be an indication that your body is working toward health. Depression can be a positive sign that you are feeling sadness at the appropriate time. But chronic and long-term situational depressions or biochemically generated depressions are very complex to sort out, and therefore, subject to easy misunderstanding. We must not succumb to the temptation to give simplistic, religious-sounding "prescriptions" for healing.

The Bible teaches, of course, that we as human beings are organized in a wonderful way. We're made of body, soul, and spirit. Christians of more radical orientation have taken a position that all emotional or physical illness is healed at the level of the spirit. They believe that if the spirit is strong and healed, there will be no physical or emotional maladies.

We all know that there are some aspects of that position that are true. Keeping the proper spiritual attitude does affect the working of our bodies in a positive way. But there are problems with this thinking as well.

Depression and many other diseases affect the whole person—body, mind, *and* spirit. The only way to adequately treat them is to have a biblical world-view that does not dichotomize our experience. If you are out of sorts emotionally, it will definitely affect your body; likewise, if you're out of sorts spiritually, it will affect your emotions. And there's no doubt that sick people suffer in their spirits as well. We are one whole being. Any complete healing plan will have spiritual, emotional, and physical components.

When depression is biochemically induced, healing requires medication. Just as a diabetic must take insulin, someone who is clinically depressed needs specific medication to reduce a particular chemical produced by the brain called serotonin.

Still, medication, in and of itself, is not sufficient. Depressed people need help to reshape their attitudes and improve their emotional equilibrium. (Our attitudes *can* affect our body chemistry.) They need spiritual counseling, discipline, and prayer. They also need to improve their overall physical health, which helps diminish the tormenting impact of their depression.

As pastors and church leaders, we must recognize the limits of our calling in helping clinically depressed people. We must respect the strengths of a doctor's calling. We must also understand that there is a kind of intense, relationship-based help that can only be ministered by a close-knit group of friends or a personal counselor.

Depression is not benign. It is extremely serious, even life-threatening. In more than twenty years of pastoring, I've ministered to many families who suffered the pain and grief of having a depressed family member commit suicide. Prior to getting treatment for my own bipolar illness, I experienced long periods of time when suicidal thoughts were constant even though my life appeared to be wonderful on the outside.

Much more could be written about depression, and I hope to do so in much greater detail in a future book. I really want to see the church equipped to minister in this area. For our churches to be healing churches, we *must* educate ourselves about depression and be willing to patiently work through its pain with those who are suffering. It is a difficult task, I know. But if we want to heal, we must listen and love.

In short, boundaries help us keep the good in, and the bad out. They guard our treasures (Matthew 7:6) so that people will not steal them away. They keep our pearls inside, and keep the pigs outside.

Henry Cloud and
John Townsend, *Boundaries*

14

Respecting Boundaries

Most leaders are leaders because we really believe in what we're doing. That's a wonderful characteristic. It motivates us; it generates enthusiasm around us; it keeps us going when the going gets rough; it gets things done.

But it can also lead to the proverbial pitfall of running a race with blinders on. Sometimes we need to stop, look around, and face up to our own limitations and the limitations of those around us. Nobody can do everything all the time—not even for a cause they believe in.

In this chapter, I want to discuss a critical subject for Christian leaders and all believers who minister to others, whether at church, at home, or on the job: *boundaries*. I'm convinced it's impossible to maintain a healing environment without respecting and observing personal boundaries—both others' and our own.

In our highly dysfunctional society, crossing boundaries of identity and personhood is common. We impose on one another; we demand intimacy; we expect disclosure. Some who go further actually rob or rape. Even in the church, we fail to respect one another as we should.

Unfortunately, people today are often all too happy to let authority figures invade the boundaries of their lives. They are more than willing to let employers and schoolteachers and doctors be responsible for decisions that they should make on their own (especially if there's any hint it would require a struggle). And in the church, believers who never go beyond the "milk of the Word" are quite satisfied to have their pastors tell them what to believe and how to live. They tend to like their pastors to spoon-feed them—and change a messy diaper when needed.

Preaching that respects the boundaries of its hearers will not command a response; it will not try to usurp individual decision-making faculties. It will not encourage dependency. As much as we might like to, we can't say, "Believe this!" (We might as well add, "You dummies!") People who have their intellectual capacities respected, who are encouraged to make their own decisions, are going to be healthier in the long run. But if, week after week, we make dictatorial demands from the pulpit—the throne—we risk stifling the spirits of our people and causing wounds to fester in their souls.

CODEPENDENT PASTORING

Many pastoring styles today, in essence, are nothing more than codependent involvement in the lives of others. Taking too much responsibility for another person's life does not offer them real help. And it gets to be an insidious habit that seeps into all of church life.

I reached a point as a pastor when I felt wanted and loved—but *loved to death*. I was the twenty-four-hour-a-day pastor. And consequently, I attracted many broken people who were perpetually in need. At the end of my rope, I called my denominational supervisor. "I'm exhausted," I told him. "I can't make it. What should I do?"

"Are you counseling at nights and at breakfast appointments and on Saturdays?" he asked.

"Of course," I responded, wondering how he knew. "That's the only way I can keep up."

He paused a moment then gave me his prescription. "I want you to announce to your church that you don't do counseling unless the person agrees to pray at least one hour in the sanctuary before an appointment and after a Sunday service," he said. "People who want counseling often don't go to God before they go to the pastor. And they don't bother to come to the services because they know they'll be getting their own private sermon.

"I want you to stick to this, Doug. And I want you to play a game of golf every week. You'll be fine in about a month, you'll see."

The next Sunday, I made the announcement with a wince. But to my surprise, the church seemed enthused about the move. I guess they wanted me to survive. The real test came that Friday night.

I had fallen asleep watching a movie, and Deb had just left me to my rest. I was awakened by the phone at 1:15 A.M.

"Hello, is this Pastor Doug?" a shrinking female voice asked as I picked up the receiver.

"Uh...yep. I think it is," I said groggily. "Who is this?"

"It's Delores, Pastor. You have to come over to our house right now. Jim and I need counseling. I don't feel safe, and I think we're ready for a breakthrough." The speed of her words hit me like a shot of Novocaine to my frontal lobes.

I had a vague memory that Jim and Delores had marriage problems. "Has Jim hit you?"

"No, but I'm afraid he might," she asserted.

"Well, I am going to hang up so you can call the police."

Jim grabbed the phone at that point. "Pastor, we tithe a lot to you," he bellowed. "And we need you now. We aren't safe together."

"Well, Jim, you can keep your tithe," I said with force. "And I have the phone numbers of a dozen pastors you can call if you want. But I'm not coming over. One of you can check into a hotel. You'll both be safe then."

"You're not coming? Do you mean that?" he asked.

"Yes, I do. Now, here's what I recommend. You leave right now and go get a hotel room. Get some sleep. Both of you take time to be with God. Then call my office first thing Monday morning and make an appointment. Come an hour early so you can go to the sanctuary first to pray. That way, when we get together, we'll be able to cover some real ground. But right now, my family needs me, and I need some rest."

"Okay," Jim said. "That's what we'll do." And he hung up.

They did make it into my office the following week. But after praying together in the sanctuary first, they told me they didn't need to see me anymore, thanked me, and went home.

In churches, boundary breaches can go both ways. Congregants show a blatant disrespect for the personal, health, and family boundaries of church leaders when they make unreasonable demands for time and attention, like Jim and Delores did. Pastors need lives too. When I told my congregation I was going to reclaim some of my time, I think quite a few of them thought that meant I'd have more time for *them!*

But leaders can also be guilty of crossing boundaries when, in their attempt to be helpful, they get excessively involved in the lives of their members and begin to direct the details of their lives. When the members don't respond quickly or thoroughly enough, pastors can be tempted to exert more and more dominance in order to make sure they get "helped."

It is impossible to be whole if you don't "own" your own decisions, your own life, and your own problems. All boundary invasions result in a loss of respect and dignity—two necessary ingredients of a healing environment.

The Bible may not use the word *boundary*, but many scriptures combine to give us helpful insight into the patterns that make for healthy boundary-keeping. I call these the "one another" passages because they tell us how we are to relate to one another as brothers and sisters in Christ. I believe that when we put these passages together, a clear picture arises of a healthy and respectful church.

- The believers are devoted to one another and give preference to one another (Romans 12:10).
- They love one another (Romans 13:8).
- They refrain from judging one another (Romans 14:13).
- They edify one another (Romans 14:19).
- They instruct one another (Romans 15:14).
- They serve one another (Galatians 5:13).
- They don't hurt one another (Galatians 5:15).
- They don't provoke one another through conceit (Galatians 5:26).
- They help carry one another's burdens (Galatians 6:2).
- They are patient with one another (Ephesians 4:2).
- They are kind and forgiving toward one another (Ephesians 4:32).

- They submit to one another (Ephesians 5:21).
- They esteem one another (Philippians 2:3).
- They don't deceive one another (Colossians 3:9).
- They encourage one another (1 Thessalonians 4:18).
- They stimulate one another to do good works (Hebrews 10:24).
- They don't slander one another (James 4:11).
- They don't complain against one another (James 5:9).
- They confess their sins to one another and pray for one another (James 5:16).
- They extend hospitality to one another (1 Peter 4:9).

A church that looks like this list is not a church that violates boundaries. It is a respecter of an individual's dignity. And, not surprisingly, it is a healthy church that is poised to offer health to its community.

COMMON BOUNDARY VIOLATIONS

It's a rare church that gets it right all of the time. Let's look at three of the most common boundary violations that work against our intentions to be healing churches. I evaluate my own church and ministry for signs of these breaches on a regular basis. I encourage you to do so as well.

1. Violating visitors' heart zones. In interviewing the people I baptize, I am often startled by their answers to my question, "Once you accepted Christ, how long did it take for you to decide to become part of this church?" One to two years seems to be the average span. And that isn't due to a lack of cajoling or encouragement on my part or their friends'. One man put it this way: "It took me awhile to feel safe and to make certain I'd be okay once everybody saw me out there."

When broken and disenfranchised people first start coming to church services, they want to feel welcome yet also remain anonymous. These two desires are not as antithetical as they may seem. Postmodern men and women often require an extended preconversion phase in which they're allowed to simply sit, watch, and listen for a while.

It does us no good to force the pace. In fact, pushing them to make a commitment too soon can be dangerous. They may simply choose never to return to a place where they feel their life boundaries are being invaded, or they may make a halfhearted decision. That's too bad, because studies show that the longer a person attends a church and the more presentations of Christ they experience (up to nearly six), the more likely they are to experience permanent and satisfying church involvement.

Slapping a sticker on a guest's lapel can be a crushing blow if they don't want to be known. After all, it may be that their marriage has just collapsed, they're still hung over from the evening before, or they are extremely shy because they have so much shame and guilt built up inside them. So how should we acknowledge and include new people? I recommend simply greeting visitors in a general way from the pulpit and making a clear statement that lets them know we respect their boundaries.

I have begun to see that the methodologies I used as an evangelist in the seventies can be deadly to people in the dawn of the twenty-first century. People today are much more wounded. They suffer from relationship wounds (consider the high percentage of marriages that end in divorce); emotional wounds (broken, dysfunctional families leave long trails); the wounds of abuse (sexual abuse alone has been perpetrated upon one-quarter of all female baby boomers); the wounds of drug and alcohol addiction, and so much more. Pressing folks for a quick conversion may have been a viable strategy in 1972, but it doesn't work anymore. It takes a great deal more gentleness to help people today.

The following progressive list gives us a good idea of the typical road a contemporary person might take to fullness in Christ:

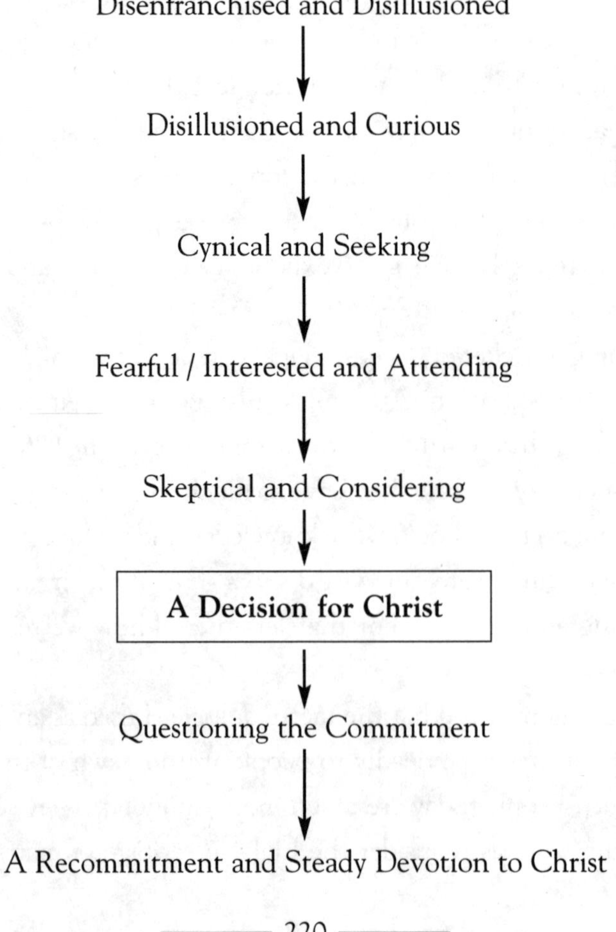

Healing cannot occur in an environment that is pushy and disrespectful. And it certainly cannot occur if we view newcomers as so many more checks on our spiritual scorecards. We must relax a bit and gently help folks move, one step at a time, along the road to spiritual maturity.

2. *Centralizing spirituality*. Time is becoming an increasingly important dynamic of church life. More and more Americans, particularly baby boomers, are attending the churches they are committed to with less frequency. The reason is simple: *no time*. Right now the boomers are the "tweener" generation. They have the responsibility to care for both their children and their aging parents. Boomer couples not only have to be concerned for one another's needs; they have to "be there" for his kids, her kids, their kids, her parents, his parents... Anyone tired yet?

Baby boomers add to their own scheduling nightmare by their dogged determination to make sure their kids experience by age six everything the boomers experienced by age thirty-two. The cultural current is strong here. Soccer moms and dads enroll their kids in self-defense, dance, basketball, piano, and painting classes. And that's just in the fall. I know. Deb and I did some of it ourselves. I was even a Little League umpire for two years. (Now there's an experience that will toughen you up for just about anything.)

Boomer parents try hard to make sure their kids will love them when they grow up. But I tell them: Slow down. No matter what you do, your kids still won't want to hang around with you much when they're seventeen.

Churches, unfortunately, don't help matters. Rather than encouraging families to spend time together and pursue spirituality at home, we tend to violate their boundaries by demanding excessive activity as a congregation. Commitment is measured by how often you're willing to leave your own home and show up at the church building. Too often, the by-product of this approach is guilt rather than joy and liberty. And people don't get healed in a church environment where guilt is compounded.

Does this mean that we shouldn't have events at the church building? Absolutely not. But we shouldn't make attendance the test of loyalty. And we must strive to find better ways to enhance the spirituality of our people, using more effective schedules that give them room to breathe. This will mean, no doubt, tossing out a lot of tradition.

But change is necessary if we want to promote health. In some families, Mom goes to the Monday night Bible study; Dad plays on the church baseball team on Tuesdays; junior goes to youth group on Wednesday night; sis practices mime on Thursdays; then everyone splits up for separate classes on Sunday mornings and goes back again on Sunday night for the evangelism service. That kind of "centralized spirituality" works against healing because it makes people sick!

It's time we take the focus off the building and work toward more outreach and home-centered spiritual growth. My dream is to announce from the pulpit: "There's no church meeting next week. Husbands, take your wives out to breakfast. Parents, have a Bible study with your kids and take them to the zoo. Singles, meet me at the mall so we can wash cars and share Jesus with people." One day I'm going to do it, and I bet it will be far more spiritually productive than making everyone sit and listen to one more sermon by me.

3. *Encouraging excessive service.* We always kept close tally on the number of volunteer workers we had in our congregation at Eastside Church. Upon studying the data, our leadership team found that

quite a number of people showed up on the volunteer lists of several departments.

There was one woman, for example, who helped in the youth, Christian education, benevolence, art, and drama departments. She was at the church night and day. Concerned, I asked to meet with her following one of our services. She was a married woman with children, and I sensed there was a reason behind her excessive serving.

"Susan, how in the world can you serve in all these time- and energy-intensive areas?" I asked. "Most people can barely manage one ministry, much less five."

Susan was already rattled by the fact that I wanted to talk with her. You know, many people believe that we pastors can read their minds.

"It's the only way I'm keeping my life together, Pastor," she stammered. "Jim and I are pretty certain we're going to get a divorce, and I'm so emotionally raw that I can hardly stand to be around the kids with all their noise and activity. Jim covers for me with them because he'd rather have me here, where we can't fight."

"Susan, I can't allow you to do this," I said firmly. "No one can serve in five ministries. And your service here at the church sounds like a way of avoiding facing some important issues at home. You've allowed the boundaries of your life, your family's life, and the church's life to be fused in a way that isn't healthy for anyone.

"We want to maintain a healthy balance here between service and fun, between ministry and family. So we're going to have to work this out, and I'm certainly available to help you decide what areas of ministry to cut. I think it would be important for me to meet with you and Jim."

Susan began to cry. She was a bit willful, and she thought her plan was best. But she did agree to arrange for me to meet with her and Jim. Eventually she gave up her "servaholic" tendencies, and over time, her marriage and family were restored.

Unfortunately, most churches have their "Susans," and they do nothing about it. Good workers are hard to find. When we do find them, we hang on to them with viselike grips.

We do not hesitate to violate the boundaries in their lives; to invade the core of their time reserves; to rob their families by taking the bulk of their attention and energy. There is such a thing as reasonable service, and we can encourage that; but too often we're blind to anything but our own recruitment needs.

Churches that heal must respect boundaries. For a time, I admit, I dropped the boundaries of my own heart and life and let them become fused with my church. Frankly, I let the congregation's activities and needs, its calls and cries for help, intrude into the sacred areas of my home. We all paid a severe price for that. But when I reinstituted healthy boundaries, I was given a new life, and the church was invigorated to depend less on the pastor and more on God and one another. We became, once again, a place where healing could occur.

You cannot deal with the most serious things in the world unless you also understand the most amazing.

■

Winston Churchill

15

Expecting the Miraculous

Jesus healed in many ways, and all of them were miraculous. We must never lose sight of this fact. On twenty-one occasions, he healed through his spoken word. Thirteen times, he healed by touching someone. Nine times, people were healed in the course of his preaching and teaching. Eight times, he healed by driving out demons. Another eight times, he healed because someone other than the sick person demonstrated faith in him. On seven occasions, he healed because the sick person had faith. Four times, Jesus healed because he was moved by compassion. At least one time, he healed when someone touched him.

We need the miraculous in the church today. Postmodern people are too broken to be fixed through simple human caregiving; they need to be pieced back together through the supernatural healing of Jesus through his body, the church.

Unfortunately, we've seen so many poor demonstrations in the ministries of high-profile preachers and evangelists of how the healing gift works that many churches have distanced themselves from the miraculous altogether. They ignore the power of prayer and the anointing with oil prescribed in the Bible for miraculous healing.

Yet people today sense they need a sovereign "touch" to escape the dungeon of their sickness and pain. So where do they go to get it? They come to the church. And they expect the miraculous when they arrive.

Whether they realize it or not, the healing they need is not merely medical or physical in nature. To be completely healed, they need more than to have a tremor vanish or a tumor dissolve so that they can walk away and live life as they did before.

The story of the ten lepers in Luke 17:11–19 gives us great insight into the subject of healing. And as the one leper who returned to Jesus illustrates, total healing requires, and is exhibited through, the miracle of total commitment.

We know that complete healing has occurred when a person's body, soul, and spirit is surrendered to God and operating the way he made them to operate. When every part of our being works soundly according to God's plan for us, *then* we can say we are healed.

I've often wanted to get inside the mind of the one leper who returned to Jesus. Can you imagine what he must have been thinking? One moment, he had a marred face and gnarled fingers, and the next, he had skin like a baby. What must he have thought as he walked down that road?

Here's what I think he was saying to himself: *My goodness, look at this skin, look at my hands! This is great! I can go home now and visit my wife and my children. Is it too late to get my old job back?*

But wait a minute. What am I thinking? How did this happen? Why am I not going back and saying thank you? This is a man of power and miracles. I must go see him again.

Leaving the others behind, he alone returned and bowed down before Jesus Christ in worship and thanksgiving. I'm convinced that's when his healing was made complete. Wholeness is expressed in sincere thankfulness. It is demonstrated when we begin to live as thankful worshipers, thankful servers, thankful receivers.

Sensing the Presence of God

It's no secret that church attendance slipped in 1996 for the first time in the recorded history of the United States and has continued to decline. Some time ago, a fellow asked me, "Why do you think people are leaving the churches?"

"Well, I have some ideas, but they're not very scientific," I admitted.

"Why don't you ask around?" the man suggested.

I thought that was a great idea, and I immediately began talking to other leaders and digging up research. Putting it all together with my own thoughts, I've identified what I believe are some of the key factors leading many people to abandon the church.

- People today are very cynical. They are sensitive to the fact that things in church are not what they are supposed to be.
- People believe that church services have no pragmatic value.
- People in general are time-starved. It is difficult for them to commit large blocks of time to church.
- The segmented nature of American culture makes it difficult to feel a part of a group. People are most easily assimilated into a church if they feel they are a part of the majority.

- Too much of the ministry is run by men; women feel left out.
- We tend to handle relational difficulties and other conflicts poorly.
- The format is often too formal and uncomfortable; people don't feel they can be "themselves."
- The music is often of poor quality, and the presentation is not adequately prepared.
- People do not sense the mystical or the supernatural.

I was reminded of this last point as I prepared this chapter. People today expect our churches to be saturated with the presence of God. And, in fact, a sign that healing is actually taking place in people's lives is that they're able to sense God's presence.

I remember inviting my friend Larry to attend our services. He had never been to church before. That day, we had a particularly powerful worship time, I shared my message, and many people responded to Christ. It was an exciting morning.

Afterward Larry approached me with a quizzical look on his face. "What did I feel when we were singing?" he asked.

I laughed, put my arm around his shoulders and said, "That was God."

He was in awe. "I knew that's what it was!" he exclaimed. "I could feel his presence."

"Larry, now you have a responsibility," I said, "to respond to that presence and let him make you completely whole."

God is the one who heals, not us. Too often, we think that we must *do* something to people—pop them on the forehead, pray a formula over them, bring them to their knees—in order to heal them. But as we noted at the beginning of this chapter, nine of Jesus' healings occurred in the course of his preaching and teaching. People were spontaneously, miraculously healed as Christ spoke, simply because Christ expected it to happen.

I believe that is one of the greatest keys to being a church that heals through miraculous healing: We must expect it to happen. If we expect to be healing churches, God will do the miraculous.

Faith: The Crux of the Matter

As we teach people to have faith in God, they become candidates for miracles. Faith was a big deal when it came to healing in Jesus' ministry. He was encouraged when someone could see the unseen working of his Father.

Now, I can already hear the wheels turning. Some readers are saying, "Oh, I know where he's going. He's going to tell us to bring the people on crutches up front, knock them over with a strong slap to the forehead, and command them to walk by faith."

That isn't what I'm saying at all. In fact, I couldn't be saying anything further from that. True healing never makes people a spectacle. Rather, healing is intended to be a quite normal and expected part of the experience of the church.

As a leader, I have made it a practice not to have a person who's been healed share it publicly or mention it outside a small group of people. Why? I've observed over the years that such an announcement puts pressure on the recipient of God's healing grace.

It also makes them a target of spiritual warfare.

I know of one young man who struggled with excruciating, undiagnosed pain for months. He and his church prayed for healing. One day he woke up, and the pain was gone. That Sunday, the pastor called him up to the platform, and the young man gave a thrilling testimony of his apparent healing. The church jumped to its feet, applauding the miracle of God.

Several weeks later, however, the young man's pain returned. For some time he kept the fact hidden because he didn't want to make God "look bad." Eventually, however, he had to seek treatment, and the news of his "unhealing" spread throughout the congregation. While everyone had prayed fervently for him in the past, many now avoided him because he was, in essence, an embarrassment; his renewed pain raised questions no one could satisfactorily answer.

"He must have some secret sin in his life," some people whispered. "He must not have a strong faith," said others. The young man slid into depression and eventually stopped coming to church. Later, doctors discovered that he had a chronic illness that was characterized by a cycle of flareups and remissions.

I don't think healing is supposed to be the center of what we talk about in our churches. Rather, I think it's intended to be a by-product of a church that seeks wholeness through Jesus Christ. When we become thankful worshipers of who Jesus is, healing occurs. It should be so expected, so natural, that it is not a spectacle. For the church, healing should be like breathing.

Listen to how James put it:

> Is any one of you in trouble? He should pray. Is anyone happy? Let him sing songs of praise. Is any one of you sick? He should call the elders of the church to pray over him and anoint him with oil in the name of the Lord. And the prayer offered in faith will make the sick person well; the Lord will raise him up. If he

> has sinned, he will be forgiven. Therefore confess your sins to each other and pray for each other so that you may be healed. The prayer of a righteous man is powerful and effective. (5:13–16)

As one who is part of the evangelical movement and has experienced charismatic gifts, I have nevertheless grown to hunger for *liturgies* of healing. This passage from James seems to make reference to a formalized period in early church assemblies when sick people were prayed for, anointed with oil, and encouraged to evaluate their lives. I'm convinced we need such periods in our churches today.

I'll never forget the time when, as a young pastor, I was approached by one of the elders of our church who had just been diagnosed with a serious degenerative disease.

With tears in his eyes, he opened his Bible and read James 5:13–16 out loud. This was my first senior-pastor assignment, and I was a little uncomfortable. I wasn't used to being an authority figure for men twice my age.

"Pastor," he said, "I want to confess that I've been obese; I've given place to anger in my business for years; I've been an absentee father; and I've spoken ill of other brethren."

I stood stunned. I didn't know what to say, so I prayed under my breath and started talking.

"I forgive you, and I bless you and release you," I said. Then I took some oil, placed it on his forehead, and began to pray with him that God would heal him.

I still see this man from time to time, and I must say he looks fairly healthy. Because of the prayer of faith and the help of some good doctors, he has become a healthier person, inside and out.

I've pondered this event for years. There was something wonderful about it. I think that's when I first started to wonder if churches shouldn't have healing liturgies: choruses and songs rehearsing our joy in the healing power of God, along with designated times within our services for our response to the healing power of Christ. A healing liturgy would keep healing from becoming overly spectacular and make it a natural part of the church.

Praying for Healing

I have never been comfortable with what I see as the "forced theology" of certain segments of the church. It concerns me when extended singing and protracted preaching with a chantlike sound are used to turn people's pain into a vehicle for validation of their faith or the speaker's faith. Somehow I can't imagine the twelve disciples strategizing to set the "right" atmosphere, singing for an hour in four-part harmony, then lining people up for "the touch" as Jesus healed. I have steered clear of such things. It reads a whole lot less contrived and more natural in the Book.

How easily culture can replace common sense! Yet there is ample biblical evidence for us to expect and even encourage the possibility that ill people can be miraculously healed. I believe this happens a lot more than we think. And despite my cynicism of the big-dollar healing parades, it doesn't lessen the likelihood that God does want to heal more than many of us suspect.

The Bible reveals an open universe: a world that God enters into, breaking nearly every law of physics to do wonderful, healing things. True, there sometimes were years or even decades between the recorded miracles of the early church. Still, healing happened, whatever the frequency.

I don't think our option is to join the crowd that promotes the miracle-a-minute, calling forth unconfirmable healing in emotional crusades or in our living rooms through the airwaves. Nor is it to join the intractably skeptical crowd that spits fire at anyone who suggests that miraculous healings can and do occur today. And my saying these things does not make me the enemy of either group! Most of us, I think, would land in the middle of these two positions.

Frankly, I have had very few of what I would call instantaneous and confirmable healing miracles occur in the course of my ministry. Yet I pray for healing and anoint with oil often. My friend Dr. Ray Vath told me that a study was done by the medical community on purported miraculous healings. It was found that 20 percent of the people were actually healed in a way that had no natural explanation. Some people look at that percentage and say, "Just what I thought! Eighty percent of them were fakes!" Who knows? Maybe. As for me, I am floored that as many as 20 percent actually were healed!

Do you realize that the healing rates of many medicines are less than 20 percent, yet they maintain credibility as therapies? That's why the medical community is beginning to pay serious attention to faith and prayer in healing.

I spent a good part of my time in the late seventies and eighties ministering in Poland, the Soviet Union, and Eastern Europe. At one point I was asked to preach in a Lutheran church in the city of Legnicia, a small Polish town near the Russian border. I was happy to go. The Poles are great people. I was there during the early years of Lech Walesa, a true hero of our century.

We sang some songs, and I preached about living in the awareness of God's presence by trusting in and studying his Word. At the end I invited anyone who wanted to be prayed for to come forward. To my surprise the vast majority, young and old, moved toward me. Many received Christ as their Savior. Then, along with the pastor, I began praying for the believers, placing my hand on their foreheads, and anointing them with oil. The pastor translated for me so I could know how to pray for each person after he interviewed them in Polish.

We came to a rather rotund women in her forties who had a visible goiter on her neck. It was purple in color and about five inches in diameter. I didn't ask why she wanted prayer because it was obvious.

As I did what the Bible instructs and anointed her with oil, she collapsed and fell back on the pastor, who was a small man. I didn't want this kind of attention-getting thing taking place, so I grabbed her to hold her up and admonished, "You can't do that." She just pulled me over on top of her, and I found myself looking straight into the terrified eyes of the small pastor.

He and I fought our way to our feet. "Why did you do that?" he asked.

"I told her not to fall," I protested. "I don't like this either."

Meanwhile, the woman continued to lie there with a blissful look on her face. I knew these people had never seen anything like this. She was not imitating anything.

Something was happening.

"Do you think we should get a doctor?" I asked.

"No, it would cost too much," he said. "And besides, it would not be good for the authorities to find out about such things."

So we prayed for the others and then sat and talked for about forty-five minutes. Eventually the woman stood up. The pastor and I were speechless. The goiter had shrunk to nearly nothing, and it was gone by the next day.

I was there, and I saw it with my own eyes. Many others who had no expectation for such a thing saw it. She was healed by prayer.

Everywhere I went in Poland from that point on, the rooms were packed. Many, many people met Christ in those meetings. But I have never had an incident like that one happen again. I do not believe it is right to try to make it happen. We are to preach Jesus and have compassion and let God do what he will. Healing is the by-product of the clear proclamation of Jesus and His mission for us. An excessive pursuit of miracles detracts from the major miracle, which is people receiving Christ.

Still, I pray for miracles. It makes good sense to believe God heals outside our natural physical dimensions. The medical community believes in miracles and prayer, so we might as well too! It is clearly our domain as the Bible reveals it.

Wisdom in the Healing Ministry

Because of the abuse and misuse of healing miracles over the last few decades, it's important for healing churches to approach the miraculous side of healing with great wisdom. It is possible to heal, and to heal miraculously, without succumbing to showmanship or other modern errors. A reckless or abusive approach to healing may actually destroy a church; a wise, biblical approach will ignite faith and focus attention on the mercy and grace of God. I recommend the following eleven steps to healing churches:

1. *Never make miraculous healing "center stage."* The apostle John wrote, "The testimony of Jesus is the spirit of prophecy" (Revelation

19:10). In other words, Jesus is what everything is all about. He needs to be center stage in every service and in all that we do.

2. *Offer regular times of healing liturgy* where people can be prayed for, and have elders or lay leaders ready to pray. This sends the message that healing is normal and expected.

3. *Have medical doctors confirm claims of miraculous healing.* Cynicism is thick enough in our culture today without us making and promoting false claims. True healing will stand the test.

4. *Don't be afraid to correct someone* who has been obnoxious in their approach to sick people, subjecting them to theatrics to confirm God's word.

On this point, I feel it is important to bring up Christian TV, where these theatrics are often observed. I personally agree with journalist Malcolm Muggeridge and others who contend that Christians on TV will always look glib and downright silly. After all, TV is primarily an illusory medium; it is a poor conveyor of bedrock truth. It brings attention to the "star," and everyone and everything else is just "part of the show."

Unfortunately, because TV ministries have tended to emphasize the phenomenal and the extreme, they've made Christianity into "entertainment," and we've bought it. People in America step into churches today expecting to be entertained with high theatrics and life-and-death drama. Anything less is a letdown.

Personally, I'd rather hear from the simple plumber down the street who met Christ while unclogging a commode than from an overadrenalized sports hero. I guess I've just had my fill of big-time religion. I really love people. I don't want to put them on parade; I simply want to meet them, listen to them, and care for them as the Holy Spirit directs.

We are too enamored with the big, the showy, and the dramatic in America. It's not healthy. Just ask Christians from overseas what they think of our propensity to "heal" by slapping people around while the cameras are rolling.

5. *Make a "gifts inventory" of your congregation.* People who are effective in praying for the sick often have the gift of faith, the gift of healing, and a high degree of compassion. There are a number of good "inventory" tools, like the networking course by Bill Hybel's Willow Creek Community Church, that can help assess spiritual gifts in a congregation.

6. *Share sermons at least four times a year on miracles* and build the belief that God can work miraculously during any aspect of the service.

7. *Teach your pastoral team about the meaning of anointing with oil.* The oil is the symbol of the Holy Spirit, and their touch is a reminder of the incarnation that has come near to them by the power of the Spirit.

8. *Teach your team that counseling and praying for miraculous healing are two different ministries.* Don't feel compelled to mix the two.

9. *Share often about healings that have occurred in the services*—without naming names—and then glorify Christ.

10. *Memorize multitudes of scriptures on healing.* An elderly church statesman once said to me, "Doug, memorize the Scripture. Read the Bible and know it well, because the Holy Spirit can only speak to you in accordance with the amount of Bible you know. The Holy Spirit only uses the Word of God to convey his wishes."

I'm not sure about the "only" part, but that's what he said. Certainly, there is a great deal of truth in the assertion that we are not available to be used by the Holy Spirit in any dimension without having been instructed by the Word of God. Commit the Word to memory!

11. Maintain a balanced environment. I cringe whenever anyone says, "I don't believe in going to doctors" or, "I don't believe in seeing psychologists or psychiatrists." I certainly believe that God can use the talents and skills of these trained professionals to touch people pastors never could. Doctors aren't perfect for every situation; pastors aren't perfect for every situation. All of those who bring healing gifts are not fit for every situation. Only as we maintain a balanced perspective about the ways healing can occur in life will we have a healthy congregation.

I have had many occasions to help people in conjunction with good doctors. I remember being approached by a woman in our congregation who had an affair with a much younger man. I looked up the guy and really grilled him. Both asked me for help.

I detected that the woman had a serious problem with depression. Depressed people sometimes look for someone to connect with, and often the adrenaline rush of a risky relationship actually makes them feel better for a while. But later, the depression plunges them into a deeper pain.

"I really think you need to see a doctor to look into the medical aspects of your depression," I advised her.

"Oh no. I don't want to see a psychiatrist!" she protested.

"Well, how 'bout if I take you to see my doctor?"

She finally agreed, and we made the appointment. My psychiatrist and I helped her understand her moods. He explained the way her brain chemistry works and taught her some skills to help her get through some of the emotional complexities she had brought on herself. Next, I read to her several passages from the Bible about repentance, grace, forgiveness, and healing. In the end, we all prayed together. She experienced a wonderful healing and a dramatically changed life.

As for the young man with whom this woman had been involved, I recognized that he was seriously addicted to sex. He'd had so many partners for someone his age that I was actually frightened for him. I also took him to my doctor, who explained to him how sexual addiction worked.

My role was more of a confronter. I showed him the passages in 1 Corinthians 5 detailing Paul's command for the expulsion of an immoral brother. "To continue in this pattern and not make an effort to change your behavior would mean that Christians would not even eat with you," I said. I also showed him scriptures about fleeing immorality and resisting sin, and we discussed his need to be freed from his nearly lifelong pattern of sinful behavior. Then we prayed for his forgiveness.

With his heart open to doing whatever it would take to change, the doctor and I were able to convince him to go to a clinic where he could get intensive help. Eventually, the clinic doctors helped him address certain issues of impulse control in his life. He was treated and remarkably healed.

You see, God can and will heal through many means. We do not have to believe that all healing is spontaneous, spectacular, or instantaneous in order to believe that God will heal. Our part, as churches that heal, is to build faith in him and to create environments where it is normal to expect a miracle.

God be in my head, and in my understanding;
God be in my eyes, and in my looking;
God be in my mouth, and in my speaking;
God be in my heart, and in my thinking;
God be at my end, and at my departing.

——— ■ ———

Old Sarum Primer

16

From Pain to Healing

As intelligent and enlightened as we like to think we are, the fact is most of us have a tendency to give pat answers to the complex questions people pose. Most of us, I'm convinced, really don't like to *think*. I could blame it on TV and our seven-minute attention spans, but from what I read in the Book, this tendency has been around for quite a while. I'm pretty sure that if laziness wasn't the first sin, it definitely was the second.

Of course, when a person's in pain, long explanations with forty-five subpoints aren't all that helpful. Modern folks are blitzed by information. Sometimes the little clichés that show up on bumper stickers can be comforting. But good leaders know they can't give simplistic answers to tough questions for three reasons.

1. It produces weak people. We only get strong when we struggle for our own spiritual growth and do our own hard thinking rather than expecting some pastor to solve every problem for us. Healing is a process that has far more intentions to it than just physical health.

God doesn't make us sick. But if through our own misbehavior we become ill—for instance, if we smoke four packs of cigarettes a day for thirty years and end up with a case of emphysema—you bet he'll use the process of healing to speak to us and mature us so that we'll make him a greater part of our lives. He wants us more than healed; he wants us whole. Weak people don't stay healed for very long; they don't have the wherewithal to go on to wholeness.

2. *It's dishonest.* Reality is too complex for us to sum it up in ten words or less. Anyone who has raised children knows that for sure.

3. *Jesus never did.* I've had some great laughs at the expense of biblical characters. It's fascinating the number of times that Jesus, when trapped by a difficult question, didn't give an answer but asked another question. When the Pharisees asked him in Matthew 22:17, "Is it right to pay taxes to Caesar?" Jesus responded, "Whose picture is it on this coin?" Then he made a statement that not only failed to answer their question directly but also challenged their own practices: "Give to Caesar what is Caesar's, and to God what is God's" (v. 21).

Too many of us, when we're tired, lazy, or stumped like the Pharisees, take the easy way out with pat answers like:

- "Just seek God, and your problem will be solved."
- "Get your faith level up, and you'll feel better."
- "Your problem is you aren't in a small group."
- "Just love him, and he will change."
- "If you would get involved in a Bible study, you wouldn't be so depressed."
- "There must be some sin in your life that God is dealing with."
- "You need to just give this up to God in worship."

Oh, please!

The Daughter of My Dreams

My youngest child, Raissa, owns her daddy's heart. She's my only daughter, a wonderful creature, moving into her young adulthood with hopes of being a very good writer. Born two months premature, Raissa's lungs were not developed enough to get her through those first days of life without damage to her neurological system. At first they said she wouldn't live, but she did. Then we discovered she suffered from cerebral palsy.

In this condition, the oxygen-starved neurological system is permanently damaged. Nerve signals are distorted, creating spasticity in the muscles and contorting them in directions that are unhealthy for the skeleton. Sometimes speech and thinking abilities are affected.

Fortunately, Raissa struggles only with her gross motor skills. It's difficult for her to walk across a room. She has overcome the malady in her hands, and she's not been affected at all mentally. In fact, she's probably smarter than the author of this book.

Over the years, we've struggled with our own painful questions about Raissa's disability but have found no pat answers. We've had well-meaning people call us from around the country, convinced that they were supposed to come and pray for Raissa to be miraculously healed. We gave in to their pleas a couple of times. But the fact was, she hated it. It was embarrassing. And many of the people clearly had too much ego involved in the idea of healing a pastor's daughter.

Of course we pray for her healing. I pray for her daily. I pray that her schoolwork will go well, that the Lord will touch her body with his virtue, and that she will continue to be the miracle that she is.

When Raissa was in the fifth grade, I arrived home from the church office to be greeted at the door by my wife, Deb. She had a look in her eyes that every husband knows—the look that makes you wonder if there isn't something back in the office you need to go do right away. If you can escape by thinking quickly, you may avoid a ticklish situation.

"Doug, you need to go spend some time with Raissa," she said with a trace of anxiousness.

So I walked down the hall, turned into her room, and there she was, my little darling, lying against her bedpost with the lights out. She was normally vivacious and bubbly. But now she looked so sad.

Sitting down on the side of the bed, I asked, "What's wrong, honey?"

"Clarice hurt me today," she mumbled.

"Who's Clarice?"

Getting no answer, I went to the wall switch and turned on the lights. Then I went back to Raissa and wrapped my arms around her.

"I love you," I said. "Tell me, what happened today with Clarice?"

"Oh, nothing," she said and leaned harder into my chest.

Now, I knew by that point in my life that anytime a woman says "Oh, nothing" for any reason, you have more problems than you want to solve.

"Well, tell me what happened, honey, so I can pray with you."

In tears, she haltingly recounted that the kids in her class had been sitting in a circle and sharing their ambitions. When Raissa's turn came, she said that she wanted to be a ballerina and a mother.

Clarice had blurted out, "That's silly. How can you be a mother when only another retarded person would marry you? They don't let people like you have kids. And how can you dance when you can't even walk?"

Now the ball was in my court. I breathed deeply and prayed softly with all my heart and mind. I realized the ultimate test of parenthood had confronted me that very day.

"Raissa, I've been meaning to talk to you about something for quite a while now," I said. "You're getting pretty close to junior-high age, and there's an awful lot of kids out there like Clarice. They won't just stare at you either; they're going to make fun of you. Do you know that?"

She nodded, tears flowing down her face.

"How does that make you feel?"

"Bad," she choked, between sobs.

"We're going to have to learn how to deal with this, honey. Do you want to spend the rest of your life listening to the Clarices of the world, or do you want to listen to Jesus?"

Of course, being a pastor's kid, she knew the answer to any spiritual question is "Jesus."

"Jesus," she whispered.

"Okay," I continued, "what's Jesus saying to Raissa Murren right now?"

She looked up at me with a wide grin and sparkling eyes. "He says I'm going to be a ballerina!"

I felt quite proud. We hugged and prayed some more.

When I finally headed for the door, I smiled and thought to myself, *Isn't that great! I bet she'll be a ballerina in heaven.*

I don't know if you have these kinds of experiences, but I have times when the Holy Spirit penetrates my heart, slaps me upside the head, bounces me off a couple of walls, and then downloads an encyclopedia of understanding—all in a matter of milliseconds.

That's what happened at that moment. In my heart, I heard: *Doug, you're a bit daft. Don't you know that anytime that little girl walks across the room, it's a dance to me?*

Suddenly I realized that when I saw Raissa I was looking on the outside, but God was looking on the inside. And in that moment I could understand how he would see her as a dancer.

When Samuel was looking for God's choice as king of Israel, God told him that he wouldn't be able to recognize this king unless he had spiritual eyes. God's choice would not be simple or obvious by human standards. "You'll know my king when you learn not to look on the outward part but to allow me to show you the whole picture," God said in effect in 1 Samuel 16:7. "Samuel, move away from the simplistic view of things."

The problems of pain, suffering, and evil really have no adequate explanations. In fact, that is the answer: There is no reasonable, rational explanation for these three things; that's why Christ came to defeat them, and that's why they must be destroyed at the end of the age. They are cancerous and unnecessary, yet God works through them in powerful ways.

We cannot offer people the pablum of pat answers. Rather, we must offer courage to face the tough issues of life.

THE JOHN 9 THEOLOGY

John 9 records the story of Jesus healing a man who had been blind from birth. The miracle stirred up the whole town. The people didn't know how to respond or what to do now that this poor guy had his sight. He could see them, but they couldn't see him in the new light. And to top it off, he had been healed illegally on the Sabbath! That really added to the complication.

When he returned home, his own parents wouldn't even accept him. They told the Pharisees that the man was an adult and they couldn't be responsible for his illegal healing. They were fearful of getting kicked out of their church. In those days the leaders taught that your church (or synagogue, at that time) was your salvation and that if you got kicked out of the church, you lost your salvation. No son was worth that, they figured.

The disciples asked Jesus, "Why was this man born blind? Who sinned, this man, or his parents?" The Lord's response cut across the conventional wisdom of his day: "'Neither this man nor his parents sinned,' said Jesus, 'but this happened so that the work of God might be displayed in his life'" (John 9:3).

I think Jesus was saying that it didn't really *matter* who was at fault. So much of our time in church is spent trying to find out who was wrong in a particular situation; who did this or that; who is ultimately at fault—as if by getting the right person to repent, the problem would be solved. Jesus said, "Why bother? The fact is that in any situation, God will be glorified if you give him a chance."

We need a dose of John 9 theology in the church today. The simplistic formula of the Pharisees incarcerated people in the bubble of toxic beliefs. Christ poked a pin in it and freed them—and us.

Healing churches know not to wear themselves out in the futile and ineffective exercise of making sure everyone fits into a nice and simple compartment. During nearly twenty-five years of praying with people to be whole in Christ, I've not discovered any two who are alike. I've met so many who have defied pat answers.

I have always felt that the best kind of spiritual guide—and the best kind of healer—is one who does not come up with the answers but who helps students probe their own souls for the answers. In John 9, Jesus took such an approach. After the tumult of the miracle had subsided, he met up again with the formerly blind man and peppered him with questions like, "Do you believe in the Christ? Do you think I am the Christ?" Ultimately, the man came to his own awakening.

Healing, I think, is a discovery. We discover, among other things, how our bodies work. I knew I had to make significant changes in my life and work when I had gotten so tired that I couldn't even feel tired anymore. I knew this was a sign of bad burnout, but I had been oblivious to the signs leading up to that point. Since changing my church role and completing an extended rest period, I am amazed at my own sensitivity to my body's signals. I know when I have been working too hard. I even know when I have not been drinking enough water! Being healed forced me into a discovery of what would make me whole.

Churches that heal must create the kind of environment where discovery can happen and people can find wholeness of body, mind, and spirit.

STEWARDING PAIN

A man who is a good friend, a leader of a large denomination, called me in the middle of an incredibly tough time in my life. I wanted him to speak comforting words. In fact, what I really wanted was for him to come and straighten out the whole situation.

But he knew God hadn't given him that assignment. His main message to me was straightforward: "Don't waste the pain." He said that phrase three or four times in the course of our conversation. I told him later I had wanted to reach through the phone lines and punch his lights out.

Nevertheless, I took his advice. Every day, whenever the pain was greatest, I went to my desk and wrote down one or more of the many things the pain was teaching me. One of those I still have posted on my wall: "I am glad I suffered so that I know I don't ever want anyone else to suffer like this." I discovered that the pain made me more sensitive to others. It increased my faith. My friends had always felt I was a bit naive, too quick to trust, and too harsh when people proved untrustworthy; now my trust was oriented more toward sound wisdom. I wrote all these things down, and I stewarded my pain.

Do you have pain in your life right now? This could be your greatest resource for becoming a healer. Churches that heal steward their corporate experience of pain and suffering. They take what they've learned from their pain and extend it as an outreached arm from God to the community around them.

Let me suggest a great exercise. In a Bible study or small-group meeting or in circles of six or eight at the end of a Sunday morning service, have everyone share a brief account of the most painful moment of their life. Then ask, "Was God there in a special way?" No doubt you'll see many tears, but you'll also see many beaming faces.

People who are afraid to share their pain will identify with the people who are willing to. As we've noted before, the best people to help a couple struggling with their marriage are another couple who've been through the same turmoil and achieved peace. The best person to help someone suffering with a physical disability is someone like my daughter, who has struggled similarly in her life and found victory.

I believe no one can preach well who has not experienced deep pain. A great teacher is someone who realizes that life is so complex that we can't even begin to wrap our arms around it.

I've noted that the longer people minister, the less willing they are to spout off pat answers for everything. They hesitate before saying a particular course of suffering is from God, the enemy, or the person's own flesh. They don't know, and their experience tells them it's probably all three.

But whatever the source, the wise among us learn from the pain and make it work for us and for others.

Once when I was preaching on this subject, I asked the congregation to recall the most painful period in their lives. Then I asked, "Who else benefited from your pain?" The light bulbs popped on in many heads that morning.

Following the service a middle-aged man came and asked me to listen to an idea he had. "Pastor, I feel I want to help parents who have kids on drugs," he said. "My son died from alcoholism at the age of thirty-five. I watched him all those years, and it was like being burned alive every day I awoke. I know where I went wrong..."

His voice broke as he began to cry. I cried too.

"You know, I can't do anything about my son now," he finally continued. "I wasn't tough enough at the right times. I just kept thinking he would grow up. But I have learned so much..."

"How do you see yourself sharing this pain to heal others?" I asked. "And how can I help you?"

"I want to take part in the twelve-step group here and help parents of adult alcoholics," he said. "And I want to talk to teenagers about the dangers of alcohol abuse."

With my encouragement, he ended up doing both. And I know he jarred some parents and addicts into action because he was willing to share his pain.

I have taken my own advice in this regard. Since opening up about my painful struggle to be healed from bipolar disorder, I have helped hundreds of people—many of them leaders—get help for their own depression. Wounded healers, even those who may still hurt, can do wonders in ministering to others who are paralyzed by pain. Churches that heal turn the corporate agony of their combined struggles into an effective tool for the healing of many.

I fully realize that I failed to answer your questions completely and, in fact, to answer some of them at all. The answers I have found only lead to a new set of questions, some of which we were not even aware were problems in the first place. To sum it up, I believe that while we are as confused as ever, we are confused about greater and more important things.

———— ■ ————

Anonymous

EPILOGUE

Remember Jesus!

With each chapter that I completed, I was aware that I was moving closer to this point: the conclusion. All along I wondered, How will I wrap everything up? How will I tie everything together and tell you, in a nutshell, what healing churches look like?

I came to realize I could sum it up in one word: Jesus. Churches that heal look like Jesus!

The true test of churches that heal is this: When people leave our worship services, do they remember the snappy program, or do they remember Jesus? When they leave our Bible study, do they remember our erudite discussion, or do they remember Jesus? When they leave our board meeting, do they remember our creative budgeting, or do they realize that everything we have is for the purpose of glorifying Jesus?

Do they leave our meetings with worries about the debt on their credit card or with thoughts that exalt *Jehovah Jireh*, their provider? Do they go home feeling hopeless in their pain, or are they lifted up by the understanding that nothing is impossible with God?

Do they leave believing that they are the center of the universe and God is their servant, or do they remember that Jesus is the Alpha and Omega?

Do they leave still stuck in the pit of their guilt and shame, or are they set free from their sin through the forgiveness of Christ?

Do they leave our churches celebrating Jesus? That, ultimately, is the end of all true healing.

The challenge I put to myself in finishing this book was this: What would you remember? My hope, my appeal, is that you remember the Great Physician. Be a healer. Remember Jesus!